Emerging:

From Coma to Presence

Emerging: From Coma to Presence copyright © 2018 by Angie Dortch Thank you for complying with copyright laws by not scanning, copying, or reproducing any part of Emerging: From Coma to Presence without written permission of the author.

Learning H.O.W. to Age™ copyright © 2012 by Expressive Avenues, LLC. Exercises may be reprinted if accompanied by proper citation.

Original cover art *OUT*, acrylic on canvas, by Angie Dortch.

Table of Contents
Part One:
Emerging: From Coma to Presence

Introduction	7
Abide	19
Kaleidoscope Eyes	33
Net of Indra	51
Through A Glass, Darkly	93
Plethora	111
Epilogue	133

Part Two:
Learning H.O.W. to Age™ Wellness Program

Introduction	139
Assessments	147
Lessons	157

4

Part One

Emerging: From Coma to Presence

6

Introduction

Dormant

In October 2004, my physical body lay in a hospital bed, still, quiet; machines keeping my heart beating, my lungs expanding and contracting with oxygen--comatose after a catastrophic car wreck. My spirit, however, kept busy.

In May 2007, one iris bloomed. Though I planted several rhizomes five years earlier, when none had yet bloomed, I assumed a squirrel dug up the rhizomes and hid them. Much had occurred however, under the surface, activity invisible to my eye. The clustered, purposeful roots of the rhizome nurtured the iris to maturity. Dormant, not dead, the iris bloomed at last. And like the iris, I now lay dormant, under the surface of consciousness, while physicians and friends and family hoped I could awaken.

When I did begin to emerge, my physiatrist asked me to describe the first thing I remembered. I said, "Do you mean here or before?" He assumed "here" meant the hospital and "before" meant before the wreck, but, I was referring to "here" as in this world versus "there" as in the other world in which I had been living. While comatose, the level of my consciousness continued, not below--subconscious, but above--supra-conscious, existing and functioning above conscious, rational, or logical thought. There are medical scans and many ways of assessing different states of consciousness below ours, but none to determine states above ours. And yet that state is where I had been. An explanation of this state of consciousness has taken me more than a decade, and an adequate description still eludes me.

My coma resulted from a head-on collision on October 13, 2004. I suffered multiple injuries including a diffuse, traumatic brain injury when my 8.5-foot Ford Explorer met a 54-foot truck winding uphill on a narrow, two-lane, residential road during heavy rain. Traveling downhill, I rounded a blind curve to the right and was struck before even registering the danger. Instinctively, my right foot moved from accelerator to brake and so bore most of the immediate trauma: a compound fracture of the tibia and a crushed heel. The force from the impact continued up my body, snapping my pelvis in front and in back, cracking the vertebrae in my neck in two places, and bouncing my brain against my skull like a water balloon against a wall. Some months after the wreck and my completion of physical rehabilitation for broken bones, I had residual trauma to the left side of my body. With all the orthopedic and neurological issues I faced since regaining consciousness, hypertonia seemed less critical until I could bear weight on my broken leg. According to the National Institute of Neurological Disorders and Stroke, hypertonia is a condition of muscle tone so that arms or legs, for example, are stiff and difficult to move. From the time I entered the hospital, I showed signs of hypertonia on my left side. This bodily expression indicates damage to the central nervous system and immediately alerts doctors to serious brain injury. While I still lay in a coma, doctors instructed my family to keep my left arm extended as much as possible. With my left hand tucked and my elbow bent, like a bird with a broken wing, family and nurses worked to straighten my arm and wrist. At times, it required a person's entire body weight to push my arm down to my side. I quote from the National Institute of Neurological Disorders and Stroke website:

Muscle tone is regulated by signals that travel from the brain to the nerves and tell the muscle to contract. Hypertonia happens when the regions of the brain or spinal cord that control these signals are damaged. This can occur for many reasons, such as a blow to the head, stroke, brain tumors, toxins that affect the brain, neurodegenerative processes such as in multiple sclerosis or Parkinson's disease, or neurodevelopmental abnormalities such as in cerebral palsy. Hypertonia often limits how easily the joints can move. If it affects the legs, walking can become stiff and people may fall because it is difficult for the body to react quickly enough to regain balance. If hypertonia is severe, it can cause a joint to become "frozen," which doctors call a joint contracture. Spasticity is a term that is often used interchangeably with hypertonia.

> Hypertonia Information Page: National Institute of Neurological Disorders and Stroke (NINDS). Web. 08 Mar. 2016.

Trying to walk with a cane (holding it in my left hand as instructed, because the break was on my right) proved impossible. My left side was uncontrollable. I could not control a cane, even one with a wide base. There were no visible scars on my left side, no brace, cast, or sling. The invisible trauma to my central nervous system was buried deep inside my brain and manifested as spasticity. The medical team was kept busy trying to keep me alive. I suffered extensive trauma to my right leg and fought pneumonia and MRSA (Methicillin-resistant Staphylococcus aureus) infections for weeks. But, rather than remain in a wheelchair, I decided to switch the cane to my right hand. Most of the therapists' expertise went into getting me standing and then shuffling behind a walker--in time to meet my expectations and the insurer's requirements for discharge. Any difficulty with my left side waited until bones healed and scars faded. Because my son, age six, and my daughter, age ten, awaited me, returning home became my single objective.

A start

"So, when is your book coming out?" someone asked after I spoke about my art exhibit and the realities of emerging from coma at a local Rotary Club meeting. "Oh, I don't know." I said. I could not yet discern how to talk or write about my mystical experience during coma so that others could read without skepticism, and a memoir without a description of that would be incomplete. Beyond ordinary understanding or standard definition lay my experience. So, in 2010, I limited the topic of that talk to my art exhibit, rehabilitation, and return to this reality; I did not address the liminal, my time in the coma. Then, one day in winter 2014, I decided to mark the decade since my accident by writing what I had held in my heart. I had a structure for focus-- my art and several journals written in the hospital and throughout physical therapy. Patiently, I reread journals from the earliest days when I struggled to hold a pencil. Journal entries resembled scribbles with an occasional decipherable word. These pages showed me a mind and a body searching for presence in this world. At times my writing became clearer so that I applied the pressure needed to mark on the page; then I saw fading ink that descended into slanted scrawls. My penmanship revealed that my effort to establish a presence in this world exhausted and overwhelmed me. When, as part of my therapy, I was asked to keep a journal of daily activities, I was suspicious. My paranoia resulted in resentment and mistrust. My therapists were turning something private into a way to monitor my activities. I couldn't imagine why, but I assumed the worst--they were just nosy. But it wasn't the content that interested them as much as the development of a consistent practice. They had a clinical way of assessing the content and reviewing my thoughts that was important to my recovery. Once I trusted they wanted me to keep a journal for therapeutic reasons, I poured my feelings into those journals without fear of their judgement. Now, the journals serve as a window into a time of extraordinary growth and an invaluable resource. My art exhibit arose in response to a profound moment that occurred as I left for out-patient therapy about two years after my wreck. The five pieces of art anchoring chapters 1-5 resulted from trying to understand that moment. The creative process that culminated in my art exhibit I will discuss in detail later; for now, understand the art arose before this book. That art exhibit was not only the story of that numinous iris, it was a visible representation of this book. Each art piece provided me a seamless outline of my recovery. The painting titled *Abide* helped guide my exploration of my unfathomable experience while comatose. The heart of this book addresses a five-year period, 2004-2009. I produced the paintings in 2009 and 2010.

About the words: Because I grew up in the Methodist church, my language and descriptions are Christian and Protestant. My experience, however, belongs to us all. If you feel more receptive, encouraged, or inspired by substituting other words by all means do so. As I share my experience, I trust you to draw your parallels, your conclusions. As C.S. Lewis observed in *Surprised by Joy*, "Experience: that most brutal of teachers. But you learn, my God do you learn." (Lewis, C. S. Surprised by Joy: the shape of my early life. San Francisco, HarperOne, 2017)

14

Despite the severity of my wreck, Amy's death remains the seminal event in my life. Until my younger sister Amy fell ill in 1994, we lived an American idyll. My two sisters and I played with puppies and ponies, raised fresh vegetables and fresh eggs; swam in a pond every summer and skated there every winter. We participated in school and church events, drove to town for movies, shopped at the newest concept in retail shopping--a mall, and saw occasional, traveling theatre productions. Our neighbors remarked that we kept the road to Owensboro hot. When a blizzard closed school for six weeks in the late 1970's, we sledded down hills and skated on ponds and split wood for fires and imagined we were like the Ingalls on *Little House on the Prairie* (a popular television series based on the children book series *Little House in the Big Woods)*.

There was a large age gap between Sharon, the first-born, and me, the middle child, and Amy, the baby. Sharon was 11 and I was 8 when Amy was born. Once Mom and Dad brought Amy home, Sharon and I doted on her, deliberately waking Amy so that we could play with her. When she could walk, Sharon and I took Amy with us wherever we went: mall, movies, ballgames, plays. Of course, older and wiser, we bossed Amy all the time,

"Wear this. Sit here. Go this way." Our pediatrician once commented to Mom that Amy had three Mothers to mind. After Sharon married and I left for college, Mom, Dad and Amy moved to the deep south. Mine and Sharon's misdirected efforts to conquer the distance determined by our birth ages with Amy were tempered by the geographical distance. Amy was able to grow up into an individual with her own talents and interests. Soon enough the distance between the three of us would be insurmountable.

Aged 24, a talented artist, Amy succumbed to leukemia in spring 1995. How do good families deal with calamity? Must I accept Amy's death as Gods will? Must I justify her illness as a price to be paid? Must I forgive God for this cruelty? Simplistic answers from clergy never diminished my grief or my anger. I never believed God caused Amy's leukemia but worse, I believed God cared not at all for Amy or for us, but remained impersonal and indifferent. If religion taught me to give God all the credit for good, shouldn't religion hold God responsible for the bad? That was only fair. When I lifted my broken heart to God and asked for Amy's healing, why did God ignore my pleas? Maybe there was no God.

16

After Amy died and my fury abated, I quit praying for years: I had been told there was a very specific way to pray. I believed that if I had prayed correctly, God would have spared Amy. After all of my years in church, all of my Sunday school lessons, how had I failed to learn the secret prayer code that would guarantee God would grant my desperate pleas for Amy?

One year after Amy's funeral I attended another-- for my unborn, second child who strangled in the umbilical cord. The night before my routine checkup, I remember thinking how still the baby was, imagining him asleep. The next day, my doctor could find no heartbeat. Twenty-four hours after that, labor was induced. I gave birth to a perfect little boy no longer alive. Forty-eight hours after the initial discovery, we buried our baby. Although my husband never wanted to name a child for himself, he gave this child his name, *Donald Ray Dortch, Jr.* Donnie gave him his name because he said it was the only thing he would be able to ever give him.

Five years after Donald Ray Jr.'s funeral, my dad, Thomas Alva Deaton, died on August 1, 2001. He suffered a rare, aggressive thyroid cancer (the cancer that killed film critic Roger Ebert). In the years after Amy's death, Dad had struggled to reconcile her death with his life and faith. Like most parents, he would have gladly died so she could live. He spent five years in a small group reading *A Course in Miracles*, searching for any wisdom to help him understand Amy's death. As a result, Dad's new understanding of ancient Christian texts proved invaluable to him and us during his brief, agonizing death.

Meanwhile, my life continued with our healthy daughter, Audrey, born in 1994, and a healthy son, Logan, born in 1998; first in a small house, then a larger house; a promotion for Donnie to district manager, then regional manager; career opportunities for me--from performing to teaching. And then one accident changed everything.

18

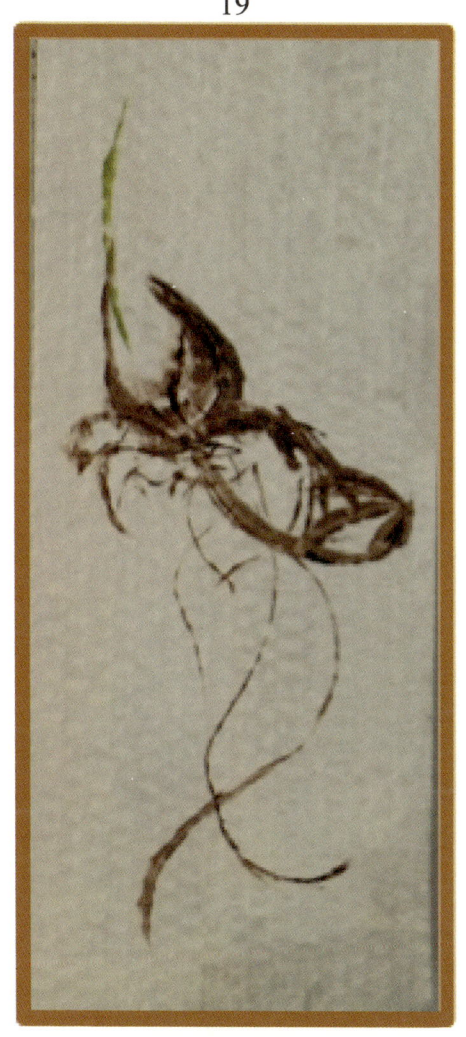

Abide

Remain, continue, stay

20

Chapter 1

Abide

911: What's Your Emergency?

  The Worthington Fire and Rescue was holding a county-wide meeting at their station when the 911 call came in identifying an accident location less than a tenth of a mile away. Minutes later, an army of qualified, trained, and seasoned emergency medical technicians reached the scene and worked to free me from my car and save my life. When I bled out twice in the ambulance, they hung another bag of blood and raced to the level-one trauma center at University of Louisville Hospital. Stuck on my shirt, a visitor's pass from Norton Elementary School read only *Angie*. Logan was now in kindergarten and Audrey was in fifth grade and Norton Elementary had been my point of departure that morning. My purse containing my identification had been tossed to the rear of my car upon impact, so I was admitted to the ER as Angie Doe. Personnel assessed my heart rate, pulse, and other vital signs, then cut off my blood-soaked jeans and wedding rings. My heart beat, and lungs filled with air because of a ventilator. My brain revealed activity and there were no signs of swelling. But, I lay unconscious, in a coma.

The Glasgow Coma Scale, a scoring system used by many medical staff, allows for a quick assessment of levels of consciousness upon a patient's admission to an emergency room. Predetermined levels from 3 to 15 tell doctors instantly the patient's condition. On an episode of *Law and Order*, a doctor explained the Glasgow coma scale to a family member of a patient with a score of 4. "Is that good or bad?" asked the family member. "You see that lamp?" the doctor said, pointing to a lamp on the table, "It would be a 3." My score was a 3: no eye opening, no verbal response, no motor response. I remained in a coma for over two weeks. But unlike the lamp, I was alive.

Initially, admitted to the University of Louisville Trauma Center as a 3 on the Glasgow coma scale, I was transferred, two weeks later, to the renowned Frasier

Neuro-Rehabilitation Center--by then a 6 on the Glasgow scale. Apparently, much activity occurred in both my neuro-intensive care room at U of L and my rehabilitation room at Frasier. Those charged with strengthening my physical body--doctors, nurses, therapists--numbered 10 to 20 at any given time. Those charged with strengthening my soul--family, friends, co-workers--were limited to 1 or 2 at a time, but occasionally groups of 6 or 8 were allowed to offer prayers for me and encouragement to my family. While my body lay still, my spirit was busy. Neither dead nor conscious, what was I? Abiding.

"Abide in Me" (John 15:4, KJV)

Beyond my awareness, God's grace offered refuge so that simultaneously and reciprocally, God abided with me and I with him. This refuge first came to me while comatose, but I sought it repeatedly once conscious. My painting *Abide* represents a living thing--a tuber, from which an iris blooms. Rooted to the earth from which it receives life, it abides until conditions are right for it to bloom. Not visible, it lives still. And so I, not visibly conscious on this plane of existence, lived still.

24

Always there was light, not The Light, but illumination. Although I could see no particular person or object and discerned no source of that light, the light simply illuminated; it remained consistent no matter where I went. I observed no walls, no ceilings, no floors; I moved in, not up or down or through, always within.

That light revealed to me deep sorrow and sadness such as I have never known before or since. I absorbed all of that sadness and regret and pain. Not a vessel through which sadness moved, I became sadness, and anguish; I sweated regret; I vibrated pain; and at the moment when I felt as if there had never been any existence but this, Amy was there with me to let me know it was time to move on, and so I followed her (ironically the opposite of our life experience, when Sharon and I led and Amy followed, now Amy led me). There was distance between us, yet we were always connected. Physical distance never compromised our connection. I felt no surprise at seeing Amy, nor did it seem 15 years had passed since I'd seen her. Amy's physical presence was just the same as when I last saw her: shoulder length hair that curled naturally, an ankle-length dress that hinted at the figure on her curvaceous frame, a sweet countenance on her face. I travelled with Amy, though without walking, or riding, or gliding. We were just where we were as needed and then in a different place as needed. I didn't know if we had a destination, but never hesitated to follow her. Then Amy stood on one side of a body of water with a strong current moving right to left, and I stood on the other side. We looked at each other.

Suddenly, I felt Dad's presence with us. I never saw him as a physical presence as I did Amy, but, I remembered him--big brown eyes, broad smile, dark hair, big dimples. The essence of my Dad, however, was palpable, and his jovial and optimistic energy familiar. He was excited and happy, and I could imagine him saying, "I do believe this is the best . . ." a phrase he often used to describe just about anything: The best meal I've ever had, the best movie I've ever seen, and so on. Tom Deaton was an eternal optimist, but never a foolish one. He remained positive despite a childhood clouded by sadness (a brother who drowned at 12 and a violent, alcoholic father) and poverty; and he kept moving forward, always expecting the best. His essence saturated the atmosphere: he was everywhere. We needed no voices and no words; we felt complete knowing, telepathic and instant. I understood precisely their responses to me, and they knew mine to them, separate thoughts, but immediate understanding.

Then, from outside me, a strong, sure voice directed me, "Logan needs a mommy." This statement was the only I heard from outside the shared, telepathic communication with Amy and Dad. I intuited Amy and Dad, but I heard this voice. This voice had no anger or malice or urgency, just startling clarity--it was an unquestionable statement of fact. As I began to emerge slowly, day by day, from my coma, I assumed Donnie or Sharon had spoken those words to me. I asked them both as soon as I was able, but both assured me neither they nor anyone else had said that. In fact, Donnie had insisted no one mention Audrey or Logan to me, lest I expend my energy worrying about them rather than healing. My loss of conscious existence allowed me to abide in a supra-conscious state. Earlier in my life, ego and reason prevented me from listening to God. But now, supra-conscious abiding gave me ears to hear. (Mathew 11:15, ESV)

Months later, when I shared that moment of sorrow and anguish with Sharon, I was close to panic. "Why did I go to hell? I tried to be a good person. What can I do now to prevent that from happening when I die?" She, of course, had no answer.

I reconcile that moment by remembering it was a moment through which I passed and which led to complete contentment with Amy and Dad. From that moment, I learned compassion, in every sense of the word. Making rational sense of that moment remains my biggest obstacle to sharing all that I experienced during my coma. I continue to seek clarity from scripture. "Bear one another's burdens, and so fulfill the law of Christ." (Galatians. 6:2, NIV)

Emergence

First, I became aware of sound. The ventilator maintained a mechanical rhythm. Click: machine pushed air into my lungs. Click: machine pulled air out. I heard the machine and then felt my lungs expand before I felt as if I needed air. Slowly, though, I realized my breathing and the ventilator were in sync. When I felt air come into my lungs, I tried to hold my breath; but it was immediately pulled out and followed by an in-flow of more air. Why was this machine breathing for me? Later, I learned that during a particularly aggressive stage of returning to consciousness, I pulled out of my windpipe the tracheostomy tube connected to the ventilator. To prevent a recurrence, doctors stitched it back in place. Of course, I can remember nothing about pulling the tracheostomy tube out, but I have scars from those stitches. Perhaps what appeared as a random act of aggression was my attempt to test out my ability to breathe on my own. Or maybe I'm just trying to rationalize an irrational act.

My nurse, Mary, who witnessed my aggression with the tube, also saw other examples of my attempts to acclimate to the conscious world. One day she found me pinned to my bed with my hip fixator caught on the side rails. The fixator was anchored into my pelvic bones with screws and how I managed to thread the bedrails through the bars of the fixator was anybody's guess. This apparatus was needed to stabilize my pelvic fractures until the bones healed. Apparently, it achieved its orthopedic goal, despite me.

A mesh-like veil was attached to my bed, a zip-on safety net to keep me in the bed and protected. I clawed at the mesh-like veil desperate to get out of my cage. I tore at the rubber collar around my neck, placed there to prevent further damage to my spinal cord. I made low, growling, primal sounds as I started to find my voice; I sobbed and screamed. For a few days, Donnie banned visitors because I would not remain clothed. Each time he redressed me, I stripped. Fortunately for Donnie, I moved through this stage in about five or six days. There was no guarantee that I would.

Meanwhile my doctors, while optimistic, cautioned my family at each stage. They offered no prognosis. Scans and test results indicated a full medical recovery was possible. Based on that, my doctors expected I would continue to improve. But what is known about the brain and consciousness changes constantly, and what is accepted today may be discarded tomorrow. At any moment they knew my progress could stop. Unable to ease my anxiety, unable to comfort me, unable to work directly toward my recovery, family and friends survived this through prayer and patience, abiding in God. Donnie remained by my side, active, the sentinel.

"You were in an accident. You're in the hospital." "You were hurt, but you are going to heal. You aren't sick. You will be all right. You do not have a disease." As I fought to open my eyes to see, I heard Sharon's voice: even though her words made no sense, I trusted her voice. I felt homesick. Unable to see clearly, I closed my eyes again. Unfortunately, I found no Amy or Dad, no streaming light, only black. When I tried to re-establish that space with them, I couldn't return. Every time I opened my eyes, people expressed gratitude for my life, said I was lucky, a miracle--"a 3 on the Glasgow coma scale doesn't typically survive." A person who "bleeds out twice in an ambulance doesn't usually survive." Each time someone spoke, there followed a pause, as if they waited for me to agree. I understood they wanted something from me, but what? Why should I feel lucky? Or thankful?

Once passed the extremes of these early stages, I achieved medical consciousness, striving to seem capable of going home. I began to realize my former life was over. Although everyone else I interacted with had adjusted to my new physical and mental deficits, I had not. Assuming where they were was preferable to where I had been, their way of communicating clearer than mine, their way of reasoning saner than mine, they imagined their world was preferable and I should want to rejoin it. But their world was vulgar, loud, and busy, a constant assault on every sense. My senses had become heightened so that every sound was louder, harsher, shriller; every sight brighter, blurrier and shakier. I suspected this noisy, flashy world kept them from life, authentic life. The peace I had known was complete, no grasping, no rushing. When I closed my eyes, I prayed to return where I belonged. But every time I opened my eyes I remained here amid the assaults: "Rate your pain on a scale of 1-10," "Try to eat, you didn't finish your dinner," " Can you name this object?", "Can you remember this number?" I simply closed my eyes: abide.

Kaleidoscope Eyes

Chapter 2

Kaleidoscope Eyes

A funhouse

As I continued to emerge, one moment my expectations aligned with this world's reality, then, suddenly, reality changed. My expectations needed to adapt to new circumstances, but I was unable to react in a timely manner. In order to function, my expectations needed to change. For instance, I anticipated moving freely in and out of my hospital room, but, when the door to my hospital room shut, it locked from the outside. I could no longer go outside my room without first buzzing the nurses' station to let me out. And, there was an alarm attached to my bed. If I tried to roll onto my side at night, an alarm unexpectedly notified the nurse who came barging in to my room, flipped on the light switch and asked, "You ok?" Although I was in a hospital room, in a hospital bed, my relationship to these places had changed. My freedom was curtailed and I was being monitored. Of course, everyone said these precautions were for my own safety because of my traumatic brain injury. Such injuries cause lapses in judgment and unmonitored patients could find themselves in unsafe situations. However, I believed I must have done something wrong to warrant this kind of scrutiny. I felt as though I was jailed for crimes, although I had no idea what these crimes could be. This was demoralizing. I was allowed out of my room only when my sitters chose, when I complied with their rules. I told myself to keep my head down and jump through their hoops. This kind of irrational paranoia is a hallmark of TBI.

The first verse from The Beatles song *Lucy In the Sky with Diamonds* became my guiding image for the second painting in my exhibit. The complete verse is:

> Picture yourself in a boat on a river
> With tangerine trees and marmalade skies.
> Somebody calls you, you answer quite slowly.
> A girl with kaleidoscope eyes
>
> Lennon, John and McCartney, Paul. *Lucy In The Sky With Diamonds.* Sgt.Pepper's Lonely Hearts Club Band. Capitol Records.1967.

When I began putting together my art exhibit, this verse kept running through my head. As I researched the lyrics, the words echoed the world I had experienced in 2004, but, a time I described as a kaleidoscope in 2010 seemed more like a funhouse of distorted shapes and shifting terrain designed to trick or scare me in 2004. In spring 2004, I literally struggled to "answer quite slowly."

A kaleidoscope produces a rotating picture which changes because of external manipulation. The changing picture retains elements of the original, but relationships among parts to the whole picture change. And, a kaleidoscope can be beautiful. In the hospital, my relationship to the parts of the whole changed but there seemed no longer to be elements of my original life. The glimpses of familiarity and comfort were gone, replaced by distorted images I could not understand. I wanted to figure out how to function in this funhouse so I could leave the hospital for home. I never imagined the funhouse was in my head, was my head.

I also wrote this next caption in response to a doctors' prediction that a 5-year recovery time was not unrealistic. This psychologist warned that I would make the most progress the first 12 to 18 months but a complete recovery could take as long as 5 years. At first, that prognosis devastated me. Then, as my recovery continued, I felt relief. I was still trying to get back to something; who I was, what I did before the injury and 5 years meant complete recovery was yet to come. But then one day during out-patient therapy, a therapist called all patients into a conference room and asked us to go around the table and tell about ourselves. Without exception, each person's doctor had said he or she could achieve a complete recovery. When the last person had spoken, the therapist drew the meeting to a close by saying, "...on a scale from 1 to 10, if you functioned at a level 10 before the brain injury, you will never function at that level again." He explained that doctors offering such timelines do not work with traumatic brain injury patients daily. But as a therapist who did, he had never seen a patient without some after-effects of the injury. Maybe he thought we needed tough love, or he was having a bad day. Whatever the reason, it was devastating to hear in 2005. So, I chose to ignore it and continued to try to prove him wrong. Now, I understand that I will never be a person without a brain injury. Doctors looking at an MRI of my brain will always see my history; a traumatic brain injury leaves a mark that no amount of rehabilitation can erase. 5 years gave me time to accept "brain injured" is part of who I am. Comparing myself now to the person I was a decade ago would be futile for anyone, brain injured or not. What was taken from me in function I have tried to make up for in wisdom. And I pray that will continue. The caption below *Kaleidoscope Eyes* read:

> *Hallucinating, conscious dreaming;*
> *Tripping, without drugs.*
> *Can I take a drug to stop it?*
> *Prescription: Take five years and call me in the morning.*

The third line is a facetious, rhetorical question that leads to the prescription in line four. This rather cynical view of my world reflects exactly how I was feeling about the state of things. Happily, I don't still feel the need to "call" any doctors. After 5 or so years, I stopped feeling like I was on a psychedelic "trip" and it hadn't taken a drug "to stop it", it had taken time.

Step by step, inch by inch, second by second

While still in Frazier Hospital, I gradually moved

past one physical milestone, then another: I stood for 30 seconds, then 60 seconds. I passed fine-motor-skill tests requiring moving as many pegs in and out of holes as possible--10 pegs in 60 seconds, then 15 pegs, then 20 pegs, and more, always more, always faster. I succeeded in a gross-motor-skill test stepping up one step at a time, then 5 steps, then a whole flight, then climbing a flight of stairs while alternating right and left steps. Speech therapy, occupational therapy, neurological therapy, psychological therapy, nutritional therapy--the schedule, the demands were relentless. For hours I sat in bed practicing the fine motor skills required for shuffling and dealing cards, a little faster and faster each time. I practiced isolating a body part and moving that one part only, over and over. Day after day in the hospital, I woke, tried, failed, and tried again. There was always something to do, something I should do, should be able to do, at which I would surely fail.

When cleared for weight-bearing on my right side, I was asked to walk a straight line. Of course, I couldn't begin to walk heel to toe without touching a wall or a rail. The kaleidoscope turned, and my reality would shift. My brain did not send the appropriate physical response to my muscles quickly enough. The challenge to walk a straight line is one I still use. In the therapy room, there was a painted straight line on the floor. In my everyday life, I find straight-lines in the way the planks on my deck lay, in the curb on the streets in my neighborhood, and in the crack that runs the width of my patio.

I found timed math nearly impossible, but excused my abysmal performance by reminding myself I had always disliked timed tests. But single-digit multiplication? Word problems that required logic and planning frustrated and infuriated me. I couldn't keep all of the parts of the problem straight. Did it really matter if I could look through the newspaper and find coupons for milk? I didn't find 6 coupons? Well, I just wouldn't use coupons, I rationalized. Problem solved. I kept my defensive attitude to myself and dutifully sorted beads, worked mazes, placed pegs in holes, and yes, cut coupons. Sorting and ranking information were skills I needed to relearn; newspapers and mazes were the tools. When I failed to complete these tasks, I laid blame on my therapists. I pouted, shouldn't they help me? I scoffed, they are trying to persuade me I need this therapy by deliberately giving me tests that beat me. I plotted, I'll show them. The next time I'll be perfect.

One day my occupational therapist found me on the edge of my bed putting on my tennis shoes. "You can tie your shoes?" she asked smiling. Incredulous, I thought, "Of course I can tie my shoes." But, in fact, I could not. My expectations clashed again with my reality. I could not cross the shoelaces. I sat there looking at my shoes and then at my hands. I could picture what to do, but could not go further. My brain told my hands to cross the laces, but my hands refused to move. The therapist saw my knitted brow and said, "Here, let me help." Though I gladly accepted her help, immediately I justified my inability to complete the task. I thought to myself, "If I had just a little more time, I could have done it. Why is she so impatient?"

Huge, uncontrolled emotions swept through my body. I laughed loudly and joked bawdily. I had no filter. Sometimes I squeezed my eyes shut or buried my face in my hands as if no one could see me or hear. Even if I didn't feel these emotions viscerally the physiological manifestations of a particular emotion--tear ducts filling with fluid, salty warmth emptying onto my face, my skin changing from dry to wet--seemed necessary. Rather than feeling a quivering chin or a lump in my throat, (familiar emotional responses to sad tears) my mouth pulled into a Munch-like scream. Because I saw other severely mentally impaired people with that same look, I covered my face so no one could see this response. A patient named Terry Schiavo was constantly in the news in 2004-2005. Every time my face contorted into that Edvard Munch-like scream, I thought of her. My inability to control my facial expressions scared me. What if I never gained control of my fascial muscles?

I had to relearn everything, not just physical skills. I had to go through a lifetime of emotional and intellectual growth, again. I sought established, accepted theories to guide me. Many of these theories relied on similar descriptions and were used by many in the health and medical field, so it would help me to decipher their assessments of me as well. The developmental psychoanalyst, Eric Erikson, based his theory of emotional growth on psychosocial stages. From simplypsychology.org, Erikson's *Eight Stages of Growth*:

Stage	Psychosocial Crisis	Basic Virtue	Age
1	Trust vs. Mistrust	Hope	0 - 1½
2	Autonomy vs. Shame	Will	1½ - 3
3	Initiative vs. Guilt	Purpose	3 - 5
4	Industry vs. Inferiority	Competency	5 - 12
5	Identity vs. Role Confusion	Fidelity	12 - 18
6	Intimacy vs. Isolation	Love	18 - 40
7	Generativity vs. Stagnation	Care	40 - 65
8	Ego Integrity vs. Despair	Wisdom	65+

According to Erikson, successfully completing each stage results in a healthy personality and acquisition of basic virtues, characteristic strengths the ego can use to resolve subsequent crises. I reasoned that if I must re-socialize again, I might experience those same stages again, albeit at a faster pace. I read the daily journal Sharon started for me and identified particular stages even when I lacked conscious memory of them. As my conscious time increased, I used Erikson's chart to monitor my progress and anticipate subsequent stages. Donnie recounted a day I had visitors in my hospital room from his office. Friends for many years, this couple was about our age and married as long. The day they came to visit, I behaved as if Donnie was my boyfriend, not my husband. I showered him with kisses and hugs. I was experiencing new, romantic love, adoration, and physical attraction. Later, Cathy (the wife) told me how sweet it was to see me acting like a newlywed. When Donnie described this event, I looked at the chart and was able to determine approximately which stage I had completed. It was this faster pace that I interpreted as a kaleidoscope when a stage was successfully completed and a virtue obtained, and a funhouse when unsuccessful. Relying on my breath prayer afforded me more opportunities to appreciate the kaleidoscope than despair about the funhouse.

Breath prayer

I had chosen the verse "Breathe on Me, Breath of God" (Hatch, Edwin, 1835-1889. Hymn #420. The United Methodist Hymnal: Book of United Methodist Worship. Nashville, TN: United Methodist House, 1989.

Print) as my breath prayer during my first *Companions in Christ* study. I was skeptical of traditional Bible studies. Virginia Watkins, the Adult Minister at the time, my spiritual director, mentor, and friend explained this study was not only educational, it was developed to be experiential. Still based on the Bible used by United Methodists, this small-group study sought to move participants beyond words on the page into integrated knowledge, moving biblical teachings of Jesus from head alone to head, heart, and soul. Developing a breath prayer was one of the spiritual practices introduced in this class.

> A breath prayer is a good example of "praying without ceasing" as St. Paul admonished us to do, and has the potential to become as natural as breathing. It is intended to be a very short prayer of praise or petition, just six to eight syllables. The words of the prayer can be easily adjusted to your heart's desire.
>
> "Breath Prayer." Gravity, gravitycenter.com/practice/breath-prayer/

In 2004, I did not use any mental energy to recall my breath prayer; the words just came: "Breathe on me, breath of God." When I couldn't remember where or who I was, this breath prayer that I had adopted, in 2001, always rose. These words were with me when I began to regain consciousness and each morning when I awoke from the night's sleep. It is this prayer that offered me refuge from the funhouse. In this prayer, the kaleidoscope momentarily returned and settled into a serene beauty.

I saw a picture of Audrey and mistook her for Amy (breathe on me, breath of God); I responded to Donnie like a boyfriend, not a husband and father (breathe on me, breath of God); the pieces of my life no longer fitted together (breathe on me, breath of God). When I felt God's grace envelope me, I began to live again in this world. Thomas Merton's prayer comforted me when I failed to abide in God and comforts me still.

> My Lord, God
> I have no idea where I am going,
> I do not see the road ahead of me,
> I cannot know for certain where it will end.
> Nor do I really know myself,
> And the fact that I think
> I am following Your will
> Does not mean that I am actually doing so.
> But I believe
> That the desire to please You does in fact please You.
> And I hope I have that desire

In all that I am doing.
I hope that I will never do anything apart
from that desire to please You.
And I know that if I do this You will lead
me by the right road,
Though I may know nothing about it.
Therefore, I will trust You always
Though I may seem to be lost
And in the shadow of death.
I will not fear,
For You are ever with me,
And You will never leave me
To make my journey alone.

The *Morning Prayer*, published on Beliefnet.com, reminds me to be humble. It reminds me to see my ego for what it is--false, not ego as it is commonly referred (a superior opinion of myself, conceited or vain) rather, to delineate my conscious, physical self from my true self--a child of God. The *Morning Prayer* offers a light touch about an important issue. The last four lines take me by surprise and I find myself grinning at the ease with which I walked into the trap of the first four lines; and relieved in the truth of the last four.

Morning Prayer
Author Unknown

Dear Lord,
So far, I've done all right.
I haven't gossiped, haven't lost my temper,

haven't been greedy, grumpy, nasty,
selfish, or overindulgent. I'm really glad
about that.
But in a few minutes, God,
I'm going to get out of bed.
And from then on,
I'm going to need a lot more help.

In this prayer, the writer moves from subconscious sleeping to conscious waking, the struggle between ego and God begins. A cautious step into an investigation of consciousness reveals debates from a variety of disciplines like theology, quantum physics, neuroscience, humanities, biology. Thus, the kaleidoscope turns again.

When Amy lay dying, I wanted time to stop; to let me catch my breath so I could process what happened. But, like a snowball rolling downhill that moves faster and accumulating the weight of more snow as it rolls, Amy's condition went from bad to worse. In the early days of my recovery, I wanted to cry, "Wait, let's just go back." I could have waited five minutes before leaving the school, a traffic light could have delayed me anything to change my journey that morning and put me on the road a few minutes earlier or later than the driver who hit me. But I could not rewind and prevent. I had to accept that the kaleidoscope of events would create a beautiful picture in which I would fit.

Net of Indra

Chapter 3

Net of Indra

Brain Fog

In 2004, two days before Christmas, I was released from the hospital. A winter storm arrived and snow began to fall. But when the weather front cleared, my perception remained in a fog. This brain fog remained until of 2007.

"When will this brain fog clear?" I asked my physiatrist, Dr. Douglas Stevens, then medical director at Frazier Neuro-Rehab in Louisville.

"It takes time," he said.

"Maybe I need glasses? Maybe its allergies?" I asked. Frankly, I wanted a date to circle on my calendar: Monday: go to the grocery--check; Tuesday: attend yoga--check; Wednesday: brain fog clears--check. Being a type-A personality had served me well for over 40 years. I desperately wanted to take control by doing something about this fog and waiting wasn't doing. If I survived the crash only to live in a partly revealed world, I wanted to understand why. For what purpose? Similarly, after Amy died I wanted to understand why, for what purpose. After Amy's death, I read *Why Bad Things Happen to Good People* by Harold Kushner. Kushner's book offered honesty I found comforting. After so many empty platitudes, his book reminded me I was not alone in my struggle over accepting Amy's death.

In fall 2001, I was invited to join a small-group engaged in a 28-week study of an Upper Room series titled *Companions in Christ*. This study transformed my life. It gave me an outlet for my grief and my ambivalence about religion; it reignited my curiosity and enthusiasm for knowing and understanding the Bible. For the first time, I learned about approaches to scripture and prayer that engaged and excited me. I credit *Companions in Christ* for introducing me to C. S. Lewis's belief that imagination guided by intellect is necessary for Christianity to become transformational (Lewis, C. S. Surprised by joy: the shape of my early life. First Mariner Books Edition, 2012. Print). It was Lewis's combination of imagination and reason, and the fearless searching in Kushner's book that now fueled my quest for the next five years.

    I tried to accept this brain fog as a kind of functional coma, conscious but not yet sharp. This state of existence is the reason I chose the active verb "emerging" to define coming out of my coma instead of "woke up." "Emerging" is continually progressing forward, "woke up" is definitive, instant, and complete. Having such a vivd experience while in a coma in the hospital, and currently this "functional coma" experience I inhabited, sparked my curiosity about the different recognized states of consciousness. I briefly skimmed philosophies of consciousness, but quickly realized that topic was much too big for me to tackle. I searched for imagery to help me define seeing in the fog. While I was trying to wrestle this brain fog into submission, I stumbled upon a Hindu myth called *The Jeweled Net of Indra* (Campbell, Joseph, and Bill D. Moyers. *The Power of Myth*. New York: Doubleday, 1988.Print). This myth provided a clearer understanding of the experience I had of "separate thoughts, but immediate understanding" (Abide, p. 12).

In this myth, the Hindu god Indra hangs a vast net that covers the cosmos. Like a spider's web, the intricate net has points of connection, and at each connection hangs a single, multi-facetted jewel which reflects all other jewels. It is in the nature of the jewels to reflect. The reflections become a never-ending dance of giving and receiving. The lines of demarcation blur. Like the immediate communication back and forth I experienced during coma, *The Jeweled Net of Indra* became a visual metaphor clarifying interdependence, perichoresis (the Greek term referring to the Holy Trinity--Father, Son, Holy Ghost), co-indwelling. Indra represented my Christian Father, the net represented the Holy Spirit, the jewels the Son. As the jewel is reflected in all others, so the Son is reflected in all others. The lines of demarcation blur.

      On that day, you will realize that I am in my Father, and you are in me, and I am in you. (Jn 14:20, NIV)

This brain fog left no clear divisions, no start of one thing or end to another, just a continuous reflection. The human body is covered by a web of fascia; the brain makes net-like synaptic connections from one area to another. Indeed, magnify anything, and you will observe the facetted reflection of one part to another. This myth helped me anchor this period in my recovery to an image and a story that clarified what otherwise became a never-ending labyrinth. So, rather than try to make this fog submit to my will, I chose to accept this brain fog as a gift. If the gift was permanent, I would appreciate the interconnectedness of everything and rely on the nets support. If temporary, I would soak up every minute possible.

In a practical sense, the fog clouded my vision which forced me to slow down. Before the crash, I spoke and moved at a rapid pace. Now, not only could I not move or speak quickly, I couldn't hold onto a mental image or think quickly. As a choreographer, the improvisatory approach I trusted to shape musical dance numbers required body awareness beyond external sight and feel, as well as aural sensitivity to musical nuances. Seeing movement and music with the mind's eye often led me to develop choreography that should have been beyond my students and my own capabilities, but trusting that mental picture to guide me always proved fruitful. Having physical control of my body was a minimal requirement. When I was moved from University of Louisville Trauma Center to Frazier, Dr. Douglas

Stevens, physiatrist and then head of Frazier, recognized my name. His daughter was in a production of *Annie* on which I had worked. She had several positive conversations with her Dad about me. Dr. Stevens remembered my name from their conversations and told my husband he felt a personal affinity for me because I'd had a positive influence on his daughter. But now, when I could sustain my mental image for longer than a fleeting few seconds, my physical body was incapable of responding. I was frustrated by how far away I was from where I had been before the crash. And afraid I'd never get back there.

A beginning dance student learns to articulate every part of the foot, and maintains proper hip alignment through feel, not sight. The walls of mirrors are helpful if used on occasion, but many novice classes are taught with the students facing away from the mirrors lest the students become dependent on their own reflection and unable to dance without one. I was now the novice and wanted to ween myself from my "mirrors" (crutches, walkers, canes). The same way that a baby's body gradually strengthens to stabilize movement from crawling to walking, I intentionally re-articulated parts of my feet that I had taken for granted for years. With 50%

of the souls of my feet numb, I used the parts of my feet I could feel, sense memory and imagination. Standing behind a chair or couch, I inched my foot and leg through tendu and degage' ("Quizlet" Ballet Terms Flashcards. Web. 06 Apr. 2016). Walking barefoot on a sandy beach or gathering a towel on the floor with my toes was also helpful. I received limited sensory input from the ground but responded back by imagining the ground, the feel of the terrain and intentionally connected every sensitive part of my feet to the earth. That action was key to regaining some semblance of balance.

I found the courage to risk failure in Romans 8:38-39 (KJV).

> For I am persuaded, that neither death, nor life, nor angels, nor principalities, nor powers, nor things present, nor things to come, Nor height, nor depth, nor any other creature, shall be able to separate us from the love of God, which is in Christ Jesus our Lord.

This assurance helped me mentally and emotionally, as well as physically. As a nine-year-old, I was asked to improvise to *Swan Lake f*or a dance recital given by the school where I trained. Too young to fear failing, I let the music guide me, secure in the knowledge that my teacher had confidence in my ability and plenty of forgiveness for the technical mistakes I undoubtedly made. That experience inflamed my creativity and confirmed my deep connection to music and dance, a connection I believe everyone has. It was perhaps my first lesson in the power of assurance. And if my human dance teacher's assurance sparked that creative flame in me at age 9, how much greater is God's assurance?

I relied on this promise soon after coming home. Emotions connected to my traumatic brain injury came on me like a tsunami. Unsure of how I would keep my head above the wave, I would make my way to an armchair. Sitting down, I literally grasped the arms of the chair, closed my eyes, surrendered my will, and silently recited anything I could think of: The Lord's Prayer, a Shakespearean sonnet, a nursery rhyme, the alphabet. Over and over I would repeat the words and let the images appear until the emotion subsided and I was again present in this time and place.

One day after climbing my stairs at home, I needed to lay down flat on my back, place my hand on my diaphragm, and remind myself how to breathe. I momentarily "forgot" how to breathe and was close to hyperventilation and panic. Once, in the hospital, I had "forgotten" how to swallow. It took my nurse's assurance to calm me down enough to let my body respond. This time there was no nurse, so I recalled my nurse's calm voice and tried to relax. Lying flat on my back, I placed my hands on my stomach. I imagined my diaphragm expanding, moving my abdomen down, making room for my lungs to fill with oxygen, and shortly felt my abdomen rise and lower. The net had been there when I needed it. The net would always be there, is always there.

In fall of 2006, after a year and a half of intense, out-patient therapy, still frustrated and saddened by brain fog, I began working with a visual therapist. While comatose, I had something called acquired nystagmus (fluttering eye movement). As part of the services offered by Frasier Neuro-Rehabilitation, a visual therapist visited the outpatient facility to assess patients and make recommendations. Since the diffuse nature of my traumatic brain injury affected the area of my brain that coordinates eye movement, it was important to exercise muscles in my eyes to avoid double-vision-like symptoms. As a consequence of visual therapy, I discovered that I had been subconsciously compensating for my lack of visual dexterity by turning my entire body or tilting my head up or down instead of raising or lowering my eyes or using my peripheral vision. I added a new exercise to my growing list of exercises: In front of a mirror, I stretched my eye muscles by rolling my eyeballs up as far as possible, then down, then left and right. This exercise was a very precise, isolated movement. It reminded me of a practice I learned about in graduate school from the book *Awareness Through Movement* by Moshe Feldenkrais (Feldenkrais, Moshé. Awareness through Movement: Health Exercises for Personal Growth. New York: HarperCollins, 1977. Print).

Moshe Feldenkrais grew up in what today is Belarus and studied in Paris for a degree in engineering. After a judo injury (he was a second-degree blackbelt), he began experimenting with a more integral approach to movement and wrote several books documenting his success. Today many consider Feldenkrais the father of somatic-movement practices. The key to success with his method is efficient muscle movement. He advocates focusing on one problem only and relaxing any tension or muscle activation not absolutely necessary to completing that movement. The practitioner then repeats the exercise 25 times using only absolutely essential muscles, then mentally repeats the movement with eyes-closed, a kind of mental practice. Over time, this focused therapy rewires the brain and replaces bad habits with good, developing healthy movement patterns. Since I had been narrowly gathering visual information by using neck and shoulder muscles to turn my head rather than eye muscles to rotate my eyes, this practice expanded my view and perspective. Although I could sense positive effects at the time I practiced (like better balance), I remained impatient.

Every moment counts

By now, my emotional tsunamis had calmed, but, I began to recognize a disconnect between what I experienced and what I felt. I observed my life rather than participating in it. Maybe, in an effort to stabilize emotional responses, my brain had actually gone too far in the other direction? I recognized that vacant look in fellow patients. Once in the therapy pool, I saw a woman walking in the pool. Her husband was in the water with her, speaking to her, encouraging her; yet, while she physically performed therapeutic tasks assigned, her eyes looked empty. She looked not at him, but through him. This was a hollow look. I knew that look. Now, when I could engage in the present, I could only sustain focus a minute or two. While eating outdoors with friends my focus slipped away from the conversation to a fly on the table. I became as engrossed in the fly's activities as I had been in the conversation.

An undamaged brain processes new information so fast its unnoticeable. The traumatic brain injury I had sustained in the wreck had interrupted this process.

My therapist labeled this a processing disorder. I was grateful therapists designated this as a *disorder*. After all, dis-order can become order. This possibility gave me hope. Feldenkrais states that "this delay between a thought process and its translation into action is long enough to make it possible to [correct] inhibit" the movement (*Awareness through Movement: Health Exercises for Personal Growth*. New York: HarperCollins, page 45). In graduate school, I learned how to take advantage of this brief delay in order to define a character. The choices an actor makes communicate information about the character to the audience. Therefore, the time between thought and action was used as part of my training in character development, first to find those traits of commonality, and then to alter my personal traits to accurately reflect the characters. Now, I filled that pregnant pause with purpose. Rather than let my mind

Tom and Janice Deaton, summer 2000, Dad died 1 year later. I can now now see the beginnings of a tumor under his chin.

Sisters Three. Sharon, Amy, Angie, 1976 and 1994

Amy. Amy Lynn Deaton before her death from leukemia in 1995. She cut her hair short to avoid the shock of losing her hair all at once.

Sisters Two.
Sharon and Angie, 1997

Irises. The miraculous emergence of yellow, bearded irises.

Dortch Vacation. Our family—Donnie, Angie, Audrey, Logan—on vacation in Destin, Florida, in September 2004, just a couple of weeks before the wreck on Hwy. 22.

Guardrail at Curve. Undamaged, proving the semi-driver's recollection faulty.

My Explorer. My crash was the first of six wrecks on this section of road on 13 October 2004.

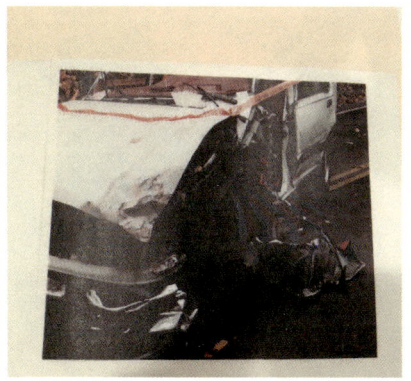

First Impact. The semi's first impact came at the drivers-side door on my Explorer.

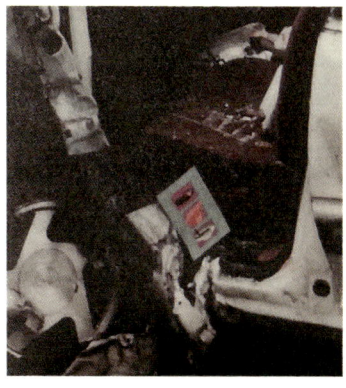

Incongruity. A sweet card from a Girl Scout Troop, amidst the wreckage.

float free like a helium balloon, I counted steps, or ran multiplication tables in my head, or (under my breath) recited the alphabet backwards or my breath prayer. When I was with other people, I noticed as people squirmed to fill the silence with chatter. But I was not operating on their time, I was operating on the time God had given me. People had to wait on a decision or response from me. I didn't need to be given more choices, or guided to whatever decision they wanted me to make. I just needed them to wait, respectfully.

This processing disorder led me to a particular driving school for persons who had suffered acquired traumatic brain injury; this driving program gave me confidence to drive again. Not that different from a beginner's driving course, the instructor spent most of the time asking me to speed up and to trust my instincts. I had proven myself in their simulator, now I had to prove myself on the Watterson Expressway. The instructor asked if I would feel more comfortable in a handicapped-modified vehicle. "No, no," I assured them. I had no plans to modify my vehicle for a deficit I was committed to correcting as soon as possible. Even though nothing could prepare me for actually being on the road, at least I felt a letter of completion from this driving school would satisfy my insurance company's notion of highway safety.

After completing the program, I typically drove out of my neighborhood in a round-about way to keep all my turns on the right. Naturally, many, many other drivers honked their horns and shook their fists at me when I slowed near a green light just so I could stop immediately if the light turned yellow. A yellow light caused me the most anxiety because it asked me to trust my judgment, to decide whether to slow or stop or continue. I was content to rely on a red or green light to tell me what to do. A yellow light signaled a transition, and transitions were hard for me. Like a 16-year-old who'd never been behind the wheel of a car before, I gradually gained confidence. Like so many activities, my level of comfort driving came back to me quickly. My occupational therapist likened a traumatic brain injury to a filing cabinet turned over, all the contents dumped on the floor. Information in the files remained, but now required organization and refiling in the cabinet. The purpose of all those mazes I worked at Frazier became clear: when my pencil line ran into a wall, I backed up to the starting point; but if my car ran into a wall or another car, or into a pedestrian or an animal, I couldn't simply back up. I had to choose quickly. Ultimately, as I began to run errands and drive to appointments, I gained confidence in my choices. The more I practiced, the better I got.

Medicine, too, isn't called a practice for no reason. The practice is based on science, but the outcomes are probabilities not promises. A lesson I learned from Amy's illness.

In 1995, we took Amy to Philadelphia for a bone-marrow transplant for chronic myelogenous leukemia. In 1995, no one knew how to keep her alive without a bone marrow transplant; although chances of survival were slim, the alternative was certain. During her stay in Philadelphia, after many ups and downs, there came, finally, an extended period of decline during which I questioned her doctor about a protocol not achieving the desired effect. As Amy suffered, I desperately questioned the doctor's attachment to a regimen that was not working. Frustrated himself, he blurted, "That's why it's called the *practice* of medicine." At that time, I wanted doctors to help Amy, not guess or merely practice. My family was relying on their expertise. I now understand that doctors make predictions based on their expertise, experience, and accumulated data; a prediction guarantees no particular outcome. Though hard to hear in 1995, in 2005 it freed me from deference to authorities. The best doctors and therapists I met were confident, but humble. After all, not so long ago, experts considered the brain a fixed organ which remained stagnant after a certain age. By 2005, we knew about mental flexibility and brain plasticity. Hence, I explored all rational, accepted therapeutic options for strengthening my body and my mind, and some irrational, unproven options, and surrendered to God-again and again.

In 2008, I participated in *The Way of Discernment*, a Companions in Christ 12-week study, which followed the model established in *Companions in Christ*. A small group of trusted companions (each one having participated in one or more of the *Companions in Christ* studies) participated in that group (lead by Virginia Watkins, then adult minister at St. Paul United Methodist Church) and continue to be invaluable to me. Practices like *Lectio divina* (divine reading) introduced me to meditating on scripture. A formal meditation class at The Barn in the Passionist Earth and Spirit Center quickly followed.

Taught by Father Joe Mitchell, the meditation class was remarkable. When I walked into Passionist Earth and Spirit Center, I recognized it immediately as a sacred place. There I found a room full of ordinary people whose minds and hearts moved in the same direction. That direction was seeking God. There I learned to wait, in expectation.

The Passionist Earth and Spirit Center was a familiar atmosphere because, in 1995 when Sharon and I went to Philadelphia to be with Amy, we'd found a similar place.

As Sharon and I looked for a place to stay in downtown Philadelphia within walking distance of the hospital, I agonized over leaving Audrey (then 8 months old) for an unknown length of time. I assumed Amy might need to stay in Philadelphia for a year at least, which meant I would visit Philadelphia more than I would live in Louisville. At first, Sharon and I stayed with relatives who lived about 30 miles outside the city. But one day when we spent over two hours merely driving into Philadelphia from their house, we realized we needed a place closer to the hospital. Consequently, the social worker assigned to Amy's case told us about short-term rooms available at St. Anna's Place run by an Episcopal nun, Sister Elaine. Not knowing what to expect, we walked three or four blocks from the downtown hospital to St. Anna's, a nondescript brownstone marked only by a small nameplate and an iron security door. After we rang the bell, a cautious voice answered through an intercom, asking who we were and why we had come. That was hardly the warmth and hospitality I knew in Kentucky. But after a few minutes, the large door opened, and a petite woman wearing a habit appeared, Sister Elaine. After Sharon and I warily stepped inside, Sister Elaine closed the door, which automatically locked, turned around, and with open arms and a gentle smile began telling us about the place and showing us around.

St. Anna's Place was a house run and supported by the Episcopal Church. Set up to house family members of seriously ill patients and run by Sister Elaine, St. Anna's Place became a home away from home for many people. As Sister Elaine gave us the tour, I noticed one of the rooms held a baby bed (Audrey could sleep there if I brought her back with me). Relief washed over me. Sister Elaine embodied God's loving embrace and extended that embrace to us at St. Anna's Place.

I felt that same energy when I entered The Barn and met Father Joe. A meditation practice was something I had attempted since Amy's death; I instinctively believed a practice of quieting my mind would help me. But with two small children I couldn't justify sitting for 20 minutes--sitting around "contemplating my navel" was a luxury I couldn't afford. Moreover, I suffered the misconception that meditation was easy. It required only sitting, and what could be hard about that? Well, a lot.

When I first started, I had no idea how challenging meditation would prove. First, I could hardly sit still for 20 minutes. To do so, I learned to focus on one thing, one thing that occurred in the present moment--breathing. It sounded easy. Breathe in, breath out; breathe in, breathe out. But while breathing, I mentally listed errands to run; and while I compiled my list of errands, I wondered if snow was forecast, which reminded me to pull out our winter coats, which reminded me of the home touch ups I had started. And so, my "monkey-mind" (as some meditators refer to it) was off to the races so that breathing in and out I relegated entirely to the autonomic nervous system; breathing was, yet again an involuntary, automatic response which required no thought. Well, then, I began again, without judgment or criticism of my inability to discipline my mind. Breathe in, breathe out. I practiced again and again. Once a day I stopped whatever I was doing and for 20 minutes I practiced. Then, I wrote down any insights or responses I had in a journal.

Once I began to succeed occasionally, I incorporated an action word to focus on, something in the present moment. *Listen.* Listening and trusting the "still, small voice" (1 Kings 19:12, KJV) is a practice I was introduced to in my first *Companion in Christ* study. During a practice of what this study termed *holy listening*, a person listens to someone else speaking or listens to the world around them and asks, "Where do I see God? What is God saying to me in this moment?"

Music bumpity-bumps, and cell phones ding-a-ling. Everywhere we hear noise. Indeed, finding silence is nearly impossible. When Audrey and Logan were eight and four years old, respectively, on our way to church I asked them to turn off the radio about five minutes before we arrived so we could find stillness and practice holy listening. After a few weeks of moaning and groaning, they began to look forward to this time and reminded me, "It's time for quiet now." "Listen for the still, small voice," I said. "What's it gonna say?" Logan asked. Their young minds grappled with such abstract concepts--but they listened.

    Now, my not-so-young mind grappled with abstract concepts as well, but through meditation I practiced quieting my own self-doubt and listening. When current interests and abilities differed from those I held in the past, I judged my current self, my post-TBI self, as inferior. My doubt insisted that, if I found interest in something after the wreck, that interest arose only because I could no longer resume former ventures; I regarded my new interests as a consolation prize, and grieved the loss of previous pursuits. I had gone to bed one night in my own bed; and when I opened my eyes, a month had passed, ten or more surgeries had occurred, and my son's first Thanksgiving Day pageant at school had come and gone. The doubt that continued to invade my mind repeatedly demonstrated my need for grace. My meditation practice provided me with a technique for quieting my mind and listening.

Disciplining my mind to listen in the moment, not the one before or the one after, is always a challenge. I didn't realize how much I lived in the past or tried to anticipate the future until I intentionally attempted to abide in the present. Sometimes when I sit down to meditate, it just feels right--my mind and body open and receptive. But most times meditation exhausts me. Like a dog chasing its tail, my mind chases some thought it will never catch. Father Joe shared the famous Zen koan about the tea cup: The Zen master fills the cup with tea to overflowing. The student shouts, "Stop! It's too full!" But the master replies, "And like the cup, you are too full of your own opinions and speculations. How can I show you Zen unless you first empty your cup?"

A meditation practice teaches me patience, discernment, and humility. It has greatly increased my mental strength and focus. I developed the confidence to acknowledge something (like an itch on my nose) without acting on that knowledge, trusting that if my mind was gently directed back to my breath, the demand to scratch my nose would go away, and so would the itch. I continued to participate in Father Joe's meditation classes in 2008-09 and studied cosmology under his tuteladge in 2010. His Cosmology class confirmed my experience of unity. Cosmology provided me with ample examples of scientific evidence supporting interconnectedness and belief in God. My coma provided me with the experience.

"We are like cups, quietly and constantly being filled. The trick is knowing how to tip ourselves over and let the beautiful stuff out." (Bradbury, Ray. Zen and the art of writing and the joy of writing: two essays. Santa Barbara, Ca.: Capra Press, 1973. Print.)

I believe we are filled with "the beautiful stuff" of Christ. Knowing how to "tip ourselves over" requires surrender, trust, a release of our ego. In Christian theology, this concept is called *kenosis*, self-emptying of ones own will and receiving God's will (Philippians 2:6-7, NASB).

Practicing visualization was a skill I developed in 1986, when I began choreographing for the community theater on Fort Campbell's base in Clarksville Tennessee. I used visualization of physical movement as a technique to teach non-dancers. We practiced visualization techniques as well as the actual movements. I wanted the performers to be able to recall the exact movements in sequence even if they weren't able to actually perform the movements yet. I then encouraged the performers to recall the image whenever they could. This mental rehearsal prepared them to respond appropriately even if their technique was still lacking.

While rehabilitating from my physical injuries, I employed this technique for myself. I decided to apply that same principle to my brain injury. In order to do that, I learned as much as I could about the parts of my brain that had suffered injury. Thanks to books about basic brain function (and lots of illustrations), I gained a rudimentary understanding of human brain anatomy and functions. One area at the top of the brain stem is the pons, and my pons had shown trauma on an MRI. I began, therefore, with this easily identifiable area. Dr. Stevens described the pons area to me as responsible for sending communication between the left and right hemispheres of my brain. When I was initially admitted to the hospital and blood spatters appeared in that area on my MRI, doctors took notice. Was that area of my brain continuing to bleed or were the splatters of blood from the initial impact of my brain against my skull? Careful monitoring showed no continuous bleeding, but therapists were cautioned that I might have sustained trauma to that area of my brain and difficulties pertaining to pons communication should be noted in my chart. Physical movements that require a change across the mid-line of my body--like stepping one foot across the other, crossing hands over on the piano keyboard, crossing shoelaces--require the right and left-brain hemispheres to communicate seamlessly. When that didn't happen for me, I assumed the pons could be the reason. I experienced an invisible barrier between the two halves of my body. Physical movement is the external manifestation of an internal process. I recognized my internal process was impaired. Although I pictured what physical movement should happen to complete a task, my body failed to respond appropriately. Whether the synapses from brain to nerves and nerves to muscles had completely broken and needed re-routing or were merely weakened and needed strengthening, I didn't know. But I believed that the more uncoordinated a movement involving alternating sides of my body felt, the more urgently I must use every method I knew to execute the movement. For example, I practiced *port de bras* exercises at a barre, practiced coordination movements and yoga poses (in particular those that required turning my torso). I needed to re-connect or strengthen mental wiring I had established over 42 years. I worked on this interruption in my central nervous system believing that connections which served me at one time would occur again.

Basic dance moves like a grapevine step were impossible at first. I practiced those and others in a therapy pool; in water, I could move fluidly without fear of falling--a danger that many people with brain injury must avoid. The advantage of weightlessness in water was a new experience. Water is therapeutic in many ways. Buoyancy did even more than strengthen my muscles. Turning and leaping in the air is as close to flying as dance can take us. When, of our own volition, we defy gravity, even for a moment, we lift both body and soul. I could regain that feeling in the water. When I tried to execute a *saute'* (small jump) at the barre or lift to the *crow pose* in yoga, my feet felt nailed to the ground. But in water I achieved lift-off.

The more I learned about the functions of the brain, the more I realized how little is known. The current picture of the brain and its neurological functions is a much rosier picture than just 25 years ago. Continuing investigation in neuro-plasticity has changed opinions and therapies. I never dreamed I would learn how to tie my shoes at the same time my son, Logan, did.

But there I was, on my steps, practicing my bunny ears. That's why the hospital therapist was so surprised when she found me trying to tie my shoelaces in the hospital. She understood what accomplishing that task meant to my recovery. Indeed, the more I realized what compassionate nurses and therapists I'd had, the more grateful I felt. All in all, they demonstrated extraordinary respect, patience, and compassion. Early on, when I had no filter, the therapists and nurses suffered from my fury and frustration and withstood my ungrateful insults. Once, I held my thumb and index finger in the shape of an "L" and placed it against my forehead to indicate to Donnie that the nurse in my room was a "Loser". Of course, she saw me; but continued her care, never taking my insult personally. I still carry guilt about my behavior and have sought to say thank the doctors, and nurses, and therapists I still see. But many I will never see again and must accept they are professional care-givers who know the effects of neurological injuries.

The fog starts to clear

From the outside, I appeared to be rehabilitating. I mean, I could do just about anything I needed to. But when I began out-patient therapy in 2005, I was shocked to realize the one thing I could not do--break a sweat, and it wasn't for lack of trying. I monitored my heart rate and at a sustained 24-26 beats in 10 seconds, after 5 or 10 minutes I should have been perspiring. The need to perspire to regulate body temperature was basic. How could other survival functions have been working, but not that one? Although my heart and lungs pumped furiously, a sweat from exertion I could not achieve. That function depends on the hypothalamus, sometimes called our reptilian brain because it is the most primitive part of the brain, shared with all reptiles and mammals. I practiced visualizing this part of my brain, firing neurons and exciting cells. I found a rudimentary brain model I could construct and re-construct. I took the model apart and put it back together countless times. Each time, I gained a little more understanding of my brain, a little more spatial awareness about how parts fit together, a little more visual memory of interrelated spheres, a little better mental image I could recall.

In a spinning class in November 2006, I started to whine to myself about lacking a towel to dab my forehead--and then I stopped: I needed to dab my forehead. Sweat rolled down my forehead into my eyes. I was perspiring! Now, 25 months after my wreck, at last, my eyes stung with sweat, and my hair dripped with perspiration. My sweat stained clothes became prized possessions. I admit, it was gratifying to recognize God's grace in a tangible way--sweat. Grace, because a human body must regulate body temperature through perspiration, but I couldn't make it happen. I put myself in a situation (spinning) to produce the needed response and then waited, surrendered to God and accepted His grace. Every conscious moment I can choose to recognize God's grace and be thankful. In my coma, I knew that God intervened on my behalf. When my conscious state was dormant, God opened my eyes metaphorically. That time was ethereal. Now I was conscious, but not present. I was startled into the present again, with sweat rolling down my back and dripping into my eyes. Again, the Thomas Merton prayer came to mind. I vowed, again, to get out of my way and follow the still, small voice. As the perspiration flushed months of stress, impurities and pharmaceuticals from my body, it also signaled the dissipation of that fog.

    The right side of my body needed to regain strength and flexibility after my dependence on walkers and canes; my left side needed to regain strength and flexibility after latent reliance on interrupted neural pathways. Each side had to be worked in specific ways. I chose to compartmentalize therapies: for my right side--the weakened muscles, ligaments, and tendons benefitted from traditional physical exercises, weight training, and yoga; for my left side--my processing disorder and my compromised central nervous system benefitted from meditation, cranial/sacral massage, breath of fire practice (Kundalini yoga), and visualization. I continued to take advantage of my delayed processing disorder. I would employ dance and body mechanics to improve my physical movements and fluidity. Many aspects of movement, of course, I continue to work on; and my awareness of efficient movement means I can always improve. In 2015, I began myofascial release therapy. Targeting the fascia, this approach requires locating restricted areas of the fascia and using light-touch manipulation to soften the constriction thereby allowing more fluid movement. Almost everything can be therapeutic, and life itself can be restorative.

Through A Glass, Darkly

For now, we see through a glass, darkly; but then face to face: now I know in part; but then shall I know even as I am known.
1 Corinthians 13:12, KJV

Chapter Four

Through a Glass, Darkly

The lawsuit

"We have an appointment with an attorney when you get out of the hospital," Donnie said, casually. "We only know part of the story. An attorney will help us learn the rest." This conversation took place right before Thanksgiving 2004, my fourth week in Frasier. But why, I wondered, would any attorney accept a case with a plaintiff who couldn't remember any details about the accident. Even then, the accident report and the evidence at the site raised suspicion, so Donnie found an attorney and set an appointment for about two months after I was set to be discharged from Frasier NeuroRehab.

In 2006-07, as the brain fog continued to clear, I found in I Corinthians 13:12 the phrase that would eventually title my 4th art piece, *Through a Glass, Darkly*.

The two words, "in part" encapsulated the veiled world in which I lived throughout 2007, and the veiled world in which jurors live while serving jury duty. During a trial, the judge and the attorneys are the arbiters of information the jurors receive. Legal arguments over which facts are admissible and which ones are not, limit the facts juries are privy to. Hardly from seeing clearly, jurors also see "in part". When Conway Trucking Company gave the driver of the truck that hit me marginal performance reviews for several years, but continued to keep that driver on the road, it risked the lives of every person on any road with that driver. Loren Fowler (the truck driver) chose to turn his 54-foot semi-truck down a narrow two-lane road, during torrential rains, rather than turn toward an interstate less than a mile away. Jurors never heard about Fowler's marginal reviews, many of which evidenced his poor judgement when operating his truck.

After he hit me, I lay bleeding, unconscious and close to death. But his first call was not to 911, it was to his dispatcher. While I'm sure this is company policy (lest any actions after an accident imply guilt), it nevertheless shows a callous instinct at self-preservation over human decency.

Moving goods from one place to another is a necessary service. Companies, drivers, even clients make decisions daily about payload sizes and distances travelled. As state and federal laws change, companies and drivers must retrain, retest, and be re-evaluated. Yet, the judge presiding over my case disallowed admission of Fowler's performance reviews and past accidents.

My wreck occurred in early fall, as leaves continually dropped off the trees and covered the roads. Then came heavy, cold rains. An elementary school, a gas station, and a garden center occupied what little land had not been developed for neighborhoods on highway 22. Because the population had outgrown the suburb, steady traffic traveled up and down that narrow, winding, two-lane road. Carved from the hill, the road simply dropped off on one side, creating a ravine on one side and a wall of rock and dirt on the other. The road had no shoulder on either side. On October 13, 2004 (the day of my wreck), that same, 1/10th-of-a-mile stretch saw 6 wrecks.

Mine and Mr. Fowler's vehicles collided. When both vehicles came to rest, his truck ended up across the road with the cab against the rock wall. My vehicle stopped facing the opposite direction, on the opposite side of the road. Bleeding and unconscious, I lay at Fowler's mercy. He testified that he simply called his dispatcher and remained inside the cab of his truck until someone from Conway arrived.

Officer Clarence Beauford, the traffic officer assigned to the bureau working accident reconstruction stated, under oath, that departmental procedure required seeking statements from both drivers; and he maintained he took my statement the day of the wreck or the next. But when my attorney reminded him I lain in a coma for two weeks, Beauford altered his statement to reflect the obvious: he never took my statement. Also, Beauford testified that he " . . . didn't feel like the injuries were going to be life threatening" and chose not to make a full accident reconstruction. Moreover, Office Beauford said he could find not a single witness--a road normally lined with cars was empty, he said. Of course, the road had been closed and traffic re-routed once the emergency medical team arrived (road closure often occurs when

EMT's believe a fatality has occurred). Yes, of course the road was empty, then.

When the trial began in 2007, the defendants and their attorneys had developed a scale model of the road and the vehicles involved in the wreck. They argued that the truck's wheels could not have crossed the center line, thus leaving Conway and Loren Fowler innocent of negligence per se. The legal definition of negligence per se is:

> Negligence due to the violation of a law meant to protect the public, such as a speed limit or building code. Unlike ordinary negligence, a plaintiff alleging negligence per se need not prove that a reasonable person should have acted differently -- the conduct is automatically considered negligent, and the focus of the suit will be over whether it proximately caused damage to the plaintiff.
> Hill, Gerald N., and Kathleen Hill. Nolos plain-English law dictionary. Berkeley, CA, Nolo, 2009.

The defense hoped to demonstrate this fact with the help of the scale models. During cross examination, when my attorney re-created the defendant's version of the wreck, the end of Fowler's truck came off the model road and plunged off the demonstration table. If that had been the path travelled, a guardrail would have been knocked down and the damage to the trailer attached to the semi obvious. But no such damage occurred. The only way for the truck to end in a way consistent with the accident photographs was for the cab's starting position to be across the center line, in oncoming traffic. What the defense hoped to demonstrate as Fowler's innocence, in fact, proved that Fowler's truck crossed into my lane and demonstrated Fowler lied to Officer Beauford. Furthermore, my attorney argued that skid marks on the pavement in my lane proved the moment and location of impact. Nevertheless, arguments about points of contact, testimony about the mechanics of a semi, and the physics of motion, gravity, and force lasted for two weeks. The defense attorney sought to exhaust the jury with tedium. The jurors' glazed looks and muffled yawns mirrored my own.

At one point, when the jury was already seated but the witness for the defense (the traffic officer who wrote the official report) was running late, rather than send jurors out to wait for the witness, the judge entertained them with a question-and-answer trivia game. When I leaned to my attorney, said this game was inappropriate, and asked him to object, he reassured me this practice was common. "Because of job duties, police officers often appear late for court," he said "The courts' leniency on this point was normal." Besides, my attorney believed the jury should see that, although on opposite sides of a case, attorneys could be congenial, persuading the jury there was no personal animosity in this case. Deferring to my attorney's experience and judgment, I held my tongue. After all, since the wreck, my judgment and emotions could no longer be trusted--that's what all of the doctors, nurses, and therapists told me. I objected not that the trial was delayed because of a late police officer, but because the judge chose to spend that time on a trivia game. But who was I to argue with my attorney when, two months earlier, I couldn't even feed myself?

Two weeks after the trial began, the jury heard closing arguments. Once the jury was excused to deliberate, Donnie and I waited. Before the trial began, I had decided to trust in a jury of my peers. Given the facts, it seemed impossible a jury would not rule in my favor--a 54 foot' commercial vehicle hit a passenger car; a professional driver hit a regular driver. The jury stayed out just long enough to order lunch. After two weeks of testimony, they deliberated for 45 minutes and declined to assign fault. The defense attorney had buried the jurors in mounds of technical jargon about tractor-trailer mechanics, and the prosecution had produced no eyewitnesses. Without an eye witness, the jury declined to find for me. Juror's wanted to be given the answer by someone, rather than trust their own eyes and brains, regardless of overwhelming evidence against Conway.

After Donnie's brief outburst following the verdict, my attorney escorted us to a conference room where he assured us of many legal points he could use in an appeal. But when he tried, the courts denied all appeals.

Almost 10 years after the trial, I filed an official judicial complaint. In a federal case (as mine was because it involved parties from more than one state), if a plaintiff believes the presiding judge's actions adversely and unfairly influenced the verdict, that plaintiff may file an official complaint with the U. S. Court of Appeals office in the circuit that governs that state's cases. I believed the judges trivia game established an inappropriate tone in the courtroom. Immediately following the trial, I broached the subject of a complaint with my attorney, and he asked me to wait. He wanted to exhaust the appeals process first. He felt confident we would win on appeal and didn't want a negative complaint against the judge to interfere in any way. So, I held off out of respect for my attorney's wishes. A judicial complaint would have been filed with my attorney's name on the complaint. This would have reflected badly on him as my representative. I still felt beholden to him and so agreed to wait. In my view, my attorney had come to my defense at a time when I could not defend myself. The cost of a trial would have been exorbitant, and he represented me pro bono. Holding my tongue at his behest was the least I could do.

A few months after the appeals were denied and his office closed my case, I was in his waiting room to meet with his co-counsel about obtaining disability insurance. Suddenly, I saw my attorney sheepishly duck down another hall to avoid running into me. I can only speculate about reasons for his avoidance, but his behavior confirmed my suspicions: He had made a mistake and knew it; now he knew I knew it.

About 10 years after coma, traumatic brain injury, broken bones, and shattered confidence, I could stand up for myself, and I would. Although the trial judge had retired, I filed my judicial complaint to go on record as disapproving the judge's trivia game amidst a lawsuit that was anything but trivial.

The Medium

Also, in 2007, I sought a psychic. Before you roll your eyes--I know. I wanted to talk to a trustworthy, knowledgeable, instinct-guided person who would share their insights about my experience during coma, but I was highly skeptical. So, I asked the one person whose recommendation I could trust to guide me: Virginia Watkins, my spiritual mentor. As soon as the request left my mouth, I started to justify my request. Yet, Virginia understood completely, she offered no judgment, no skepticism, no pandering tone of voice, and knew exactly the right person. Virginia recommended Leigh Ann Loggins. Unsure whom or what I would find, I walked up the steps of Leigh Ann's apartment, knocked on the door, and met a young woman accompanied by her friendly dog. She shook my hand and welcomed me. Then, before I said a word, Leigh Ann remarked, "I've never met someone who has one foot in this world and one foot in the other." Taken aback, I realized that was precisely how I felt--not quite here, not quite there. I briefly explained my car wreck and injuries and then spoke at some length about being in a coma. "Why can't I retain my awareness of that existence and still be present here?" I asked. "I think you know the answer to that," she said. Actually, I did: trying to exist in two places at once, I was never present in either. "Logan needs a mommy." The strong sure words echoed in my head again. As I told Leigh Ann about my coma, she listened quietly. We talked about Amy and Dad. I drew totem cards from a deck and we talked about what the significance of each card might be to me, and then I left. It wasn't blasphemous or spooky or strange. It was thought provoking, respectful and welcomed. I'm not suggesting that there are no charlatans seeking to fleece unsuspecting dupes. Merely, that an ethical conduit with spiritual insight can be a valuable aid in self-examination and growth. I didn't need her to confirm or deny my experience, I know what I experienced. It was simply a relief to openly discuss it with someone who appreciated the importance.

Through a glass

In spring 2007, I noticed a single iris had bloomed in a garden beside my front walk. When no flowers had emerged after my initial planting in 1999, I chalked their absence up to my gardening inexperience. Maybe I planted the rhizomes too deep or not deep enough;

maybe the clay soil was too hard; maybe a squirrel had confiscated the rhizomes, leaving my small garden bare. Yet, the day I saw the single, yellow, bearded iris, I realized the fog over my brain had burned away. If a purification process had started with perspiration in spinning class that day, the process completed with this gorgeous iris that demanded I see it clearly, and I could obey. The glass through which I looked was no longer dark.

In 2007, I was still receiving physical therapy. Each surgery to improve my mobility and correct alignment problems meant 6 or more weeks of cast and crutches, and that meant 12 weeks of physical therapy each time. One day, on my way to my car to go to therapy, one of the wheels of my walker ran off the sidewalk and into a small patch of earth beside my porch. In 1999, I had planted five rhizomes in that spot, but nothing bloomed for seven years--until now. There it was--a single, yellow, bearded iris. It was daring me to pass without noticing. It demanded my attention; its beauty demanded recognition. That iris was beautiful indeed, and more; sublime, and more. The iris was numinous. In *The Idea of the Holy,* German theologian Rudolf Otto characterizes "the numinous as the holy (i.e.,

God), minus its moral and rational aspects" (*Rudolf Otto, The Idea of the Holy 1: Summary." Bytrentsacred.co.uk. Web. 29 Feb. 2016*).

I don't recall how long I stood mesmerized by that iris before realizing someone waited for me to get into the car. I said nothing about the iris and proceeded to physical therapy as usual. But, the energy that infused that iris rose in me. For the next month or so, that flower encouraged me each time I left for therapy and welcomed me home each time I returned. "Look at me! I am here!" it shouted.

This yellow, bearded iris displayed God's presence, grace, love. When I needed encouragement, I recalled how the iris stood tall and straight despite strong wind or pounding rain. When all I wanted to do was lie down and sleep, this iris became my assurance that I could persevere. Then, in 2008, that rhizome, along with two others bloomed in spring and again in fall--double-blooming irises. I hoped the remaining two rhizomes, as yet non-blooming, remained alive as well and wondered why these three rhizomes suddenly emerged and when might the other two. I hoped I could unearth the three rhizomes that had bloomed, divide them, and the offspring would be as numinous as the first. That sounded risky. How greedy was I? After seven or eight years, three irises had finally bloomed. What if my digging and splitting the rhizomes killed them? The second and third irises were equally as stunning as the first, but their impact did not have the mystical nature of the first. Not only did I want to cling to the few flowers I had, but also I wanted each new iris to display the holy spirit as I experienced in the first. I chastised myself for daring to impose my human desires on what had become, for me, a gift from God. And yet, I dared. If what I read about these cultivars was accurate, divided rhizomes were actually healthier and more prolific than ones that were crowded. And if I truly believed what I had learned and practiced, the desire to cultivate and spread this seed also came from God. And if I was wrong, I believed God would forgive me the error. As Merton prayed,

>... the fact that I think
>I am following Your will
>Does not mean that I am actually doing so.
>But I believe
>That the desire to please You does in fact

please You.

 I was grateful for the encouragement that first flower

gave me and now, as I replanted the divided rhizomes, I needed to surrender--again.

I continued to plan on cultivating the rhizomes all spring and fall. Finally, on one of the last warmish days in November, I removed the top layer of soil and mulch hoping to lift the three rhizomes that had bloomed and spilt off three more. The roots of the rhizomes were a tangled mass. I started to worry again. If I forced the roots apart, they would break. I reminded myself of what I had sought to learn through meditation and centering prayer and more directly, my recent rehab experience: stop forcing, surrender. I recalled those days of returning to this world when I didn't remember how I breathed and then swallowed and then grasped a fork and then sat up. God moved me. Indeed, while others raved at my accomplishments and my determination, I knew it was not me; it was all God. Similarly, now I didn't need to steel my resolve or worry that I might harm the rhizome, I needed to surrender. That first iris was not simply a flower. Its numinous energy infused me, it, everything. It had purpose as I had purpose if I could just get out of my way.

Consequently, I took a deep breath and surrendered my will, which meant controlling that little patch of flowers, and clung instead to what I discerned as God's will, and what I found shocked, surprised, humbled me. There, just below the surface, waiting to emerge were 15 or 20 rhizomes in various stages of readiness. Tears rolled down my cheeks. Immediately, I remembered the miracle of feeding the five thousand (Matt. 14:13-21, KJV). As I gently began to loosen the roots from the ground, the roots effortlessly released their hold. After lifting the first rhizome, I noticed the primary roots were three times the length of the rhizome and obviously ran deep into the earth searching for sustenance.

I photographed the flower bed and rhizomes. Logan helped me unearth and clean each one. I became obsessed. Each rhizome must become the best iris. I must coddle and control and monitor growth; I must give the exact amount of food and fertilizer needed. I must divide the rhizomes and re-plant them. There were so many, I wouldn't have room for all of them in my garden, I worried. Stop. Wait. Listen. Discern. Hadn't I just been shown the boundless gifts that are waiting for me when I surrender my will and trust God? I put the rest of the rhizomes in a cardboard box, covered them with mulch and stored them in my garage and waited.

One morning, the following spring 2009, I woke with the desire to draw that first iris. I found a particle board once the backing for a kid-sized easel. At about 36 by 30 inches, it was big and sturdy. On that surface, I began to sketch that first iris. How could I show the intensity of this flower? From one of my photographs, I cropped and enlarged the frame to focus on the flower. I noticed the petals, though they looked delicate and light, drew support from a ribcage of sorts. I learned the caterpillar-like extensions from the center were called the beard. I saw a spider nestled in the center of the flower and included it in the composition as well. Again, flowers bloomed outside and I touched the ruffled petals and tenacious stems. I snapped more photographs of the iris garden from every angle, at every time, daylight to dusk. God's still, small voice was pulling me in a direction I had never gone, but I followed and trusted.

Plethora

Chapter 5

Plethora

"Coming out of the dark, I finally see the light now, It's shining on me." (Estefan, Gloria. *Into the Light*. Sony, 1991)

With the lawsuit's end and therapy over, in 2008, I began to look to the future. I compared the direction my life was headed now to where it had been headed before the wreck. Physically, I couldn't return to physically demanding jobs like choreography or teaching dance. My work with young people had relied on demonstration of movements which I could no longer execute. My ankle fusion saved my foot from amputation, but limited movement. The ankle flexibility we use to balance and walk was gone. The arches of both my feet were too weak to smoothly lift my feet, much less turn or leap or jump. My pelvic and neck fractures limited range of motion further. A compromised central nervous system made fluid movement impossible. A traumatic brain injury leaves unseen scars and unexpected challenges. Stamina, focus, concentration and memory were all abilities I had to retool. I felt compelled to communicate all that had happened and what I had gleaned from this experience. But how?

C.S. Lewis believed imagination and reason complimented one another. Since the wreck, I successfully lived my life by developing the habit of justifying every decision I made with reasoned, expert-guided and evidence-based support. This left-brained approach was safe. Finding a balance between imagination and reason had long been a goal of mine. In 1992, I subtitled my graduate school thesis "The Balancing Act". In 2008, the challenge was even greater. During an interview, journalist Martha SherrillI of *The Washington Post* describes Jodie Foster's acting technique as, "The duel between freedom and control. The tango of life" (Sherrill, Martha "THE REIN OF JODIE FOSTER; Offscreen, She's In Charge. On Camera, She's Learned Not to Be." 25 Dec. 1994. The Washington Post. 25 Dec. 1994. Web. 2016). It was time for me to learn to tango again.

Step One

I had enjoyed teaching and speaking, had moderate success writing and producing plays for kids at church, but my first foray into speaking in public was rough. Upward Sports is a program for kids that connects lessons learned from team sports with biblical lessons. Kids who participated were accompanied to games by parents, siblings, and extended family. While the team went to the locker room at half-time, spectators remained in the gym to listen to a devotional. I was asked to give a short devotion at an Upward basketball game at my church. I said yes, before I had the chance to talk myself out of it, but I worried. What if I could not remember what I had planned to say, or a particular word my mind searched for never came? The voice I had used to sing, recite lines, and define characters when storytelling was unrecognizable. Intubation had saved my life and a tracheostomy had prevented serious infection in my lungs, but my delicate vocal folds were traumatized just the same. Temporary paralysis often made it impossible to phonate, and getting the message from my brain to the nerves that stimulated the vocal folds took singular focus. What once had been second nature was now robotic. I prepared the only way I had ever prepared, I scripted the devotional and practiced in front of my mirror at home, but when the time came I was scared. I had to consciously remind myself to stand with my weight on both feet, hold the microphone in one hand and the script in the other, inhale from my diaphragm, swallow saliva to wet my dry throat, read the first line, repeat. I read straight from my prepared devotion, never looked up to make eye contact, never varied my pitch or intonation. I made every rookie mistake I had been trained not to make. It was as if I had never been in front of an audience before: reason--1, imagination--0. Whether or not my TBI loss was reparable wasn't known, and after my Upward devotion, my confidence in a full recovery was shaken. The outpatient therapists' prediction seemed to be coming true (if you functioned at a level 10 before the brain injury, you will never function at that level again) and my continued resistance against it seemed futile. I could no longer prepare the same way as before because I was not the same.

Around this time, I was introduced to this Irish prayer, St. Patrick's Breastplate, set to music by Shaun Davey and Rita Connolly in April 2012. It is currently available on YouTube.

The Deers Cry

116

Anon. 8th Century: Translated from old Irish by Kuno Meyer.

I arise today

Through the strength of Heaven
Light of sun
Radiance of moon
Splendor of fire
Speed of lightning
Swiftness of wind
Depth of the sea
Stability of earth
Firmness of rock

I arise today

Through Gods strength to pilot me
Gods eye to look before me
Gods wisdom to guide me
Gods way to lie before me
Gods shield to protect me

From all who shall wish me ill
Afar and anear
Alone and in a multitude
Against every cruel
Merciless power
That may oppose my body and soul

Christ with me, Christ before me,
Christ behind me, Christ in me,

Christ beneath me, Christ above me,
Christ on my right, Christ on my left,

Christ when I lie down, Christ when I sit down,
Christ when I arise, Christ to shield me

Christ in the heart of everyone who thinks of me,
Christ in the mouth of everyone who speaks of me
I arise today.

I began playing this before sitting down to meditate and before long, this prayer made its way into my life. I still prepared notes and practiced in front of my mirror, but rather than remind myself of all the technical aspects and do's and don'ts, when I rose to speak to different groups, I prayed "God, be in my mouth and in my mind." And each time, the words were available, my voice was clear, and my heart was full. If I wanted to advance spiritually, mentally and physically; if I wanted to take advantage of my past training and communicate in a creative way, I must listen to the "still small voice" and abide in God. Making myself a servant to God's agenda rather than worry about communicating my own agenda in my own way was another reminder to surrender.

This covenant prayer (adapted from the English Puritan Richard Alleine) by John Wesley, founder of United Methodism, always seemed like a list of do's and should's. But now, I no longer viewed this covenant as stifling as I once did in high school. As I surrendered to God's promptings, I found freedom in Wesley's covenant:

> I am no longer my own, but yours.
> Put me to what you will, rank me with whom you will;
> put me to doing, put me to suffering;
> let me be employed for you, or laid aside for you;
> exalted for you, or brought low for you;
> let me be full,
> let me be empty;
> let me have all things,
> let me have nothing:
> I freely and wholeheartedly yield all things
> to your pleasure and disposal.
> And now, glorious and blessed God,
> Father, Son, and Holy Spirit,
> You are mine and I am yours. So be it.
> And the covenant now made on earth, let it be ratified in heaven.
> Amen.

It takes a great deal of mental flexibility to alternate between imagination and reason, that kind of flexibility has always been hard and now it seemed impossible. In graduate school, I had learned to surrender to my instincts during improvisation; to give up the habit of pre-planning and controlling my responses and allow myself to react and respond in the moment. This approach was creatively stimulating. From an actor's perspective, uninhibited responses help flesh out a character. But now, this technique frightened me, precisely because of its unpredictability. I made rational decisions on a daily basis, but the mistrust by others I faced during that time in the hospital (when doctors and therapists required me to justify every decision I made, and doors automatically locked behind me) had become ingrained in me. My medical team, with good reason, had monitored me for lapses in judgement so often seen in TBI patients. I believe the mental flexibility I exercised in graduate school is largely responsible for my mental recovery. So, how would I now balance two seemingly dichotomous concepts: imagination and reason? Daily, I surrender control to God, an intentional choice, a constant reminder. I surrender to the Alpha and the Omega (Revelations 22:13, NASB), the example of the possibility of holding a dichotomy. Although God's grace comes freely to us, I know I must choose to accept it and act on it and if I do, I will never be left wanting. Paul says we must pray without ceasing (1 Thessalonians 5:17, KJV). For me, abiding in God through all of my life constitutes unceasing prayer, especially the prayer of discernment--and I think again of Merton.

Step Two

In 2009 when I began drawing the Iris, I couldn't justify this action but I felt inspired, and it felt good. Although drawing and painting were Amy's strengths, not mine--I drew and painted. First, I tried to sketch dreams I had written down in journals, then moments in the hospital, then coma. But before long, I became frustrated with my inability to draw my insights. My insecurities about my artistic ability reared its ugly head again. Once at about age 13, I presented Mom with a picture of a tear-drop eyed girl placing a letter in a mailbox. The original was on the front of a greeting card I'd purchased. "Did you draw that?" she asked. "Yes," I fibbed. "That's beautiful and it looks exactly like the picture on the card," she marveled. Later she showed it to my father and my sisters. I enjoyed the attention and praise, but ultimately couldn't withstand the guilt of the lie. Finally, I confessed that I had traced the picture and braced for the disappointed looks on my parents faces. My insecurities ran deep. So, when I responded to a call for artists I had heard on the radio, I did so not knowing what would happen, and not knowing a plethora of ideas would coalesce.

I hungered for knowledge and new experiences, a hunger I had not felt since Amy's death. No longer fearful of the future and the unexpected, I trusted God would gird me. I picked up a paintbrush and began to paint the iris I had drawn on the board. I used some acrylic paint I already had. Because acrylic paint dried quickly, I painted quickly. This time restriction encouraged me to paint instinctively. Acrylic paint didn't allow me the time to think through a solution, I had to act, and to act meant I had to trust instincts.

I also spent time in meditation, cultivating an awareness of my dependence on God. If a simple flower serves God, could I? I had received the gift of surrender during my coma. Although I wanted to surrender when conscious, my ego prevented me. After years of hearing from physicians and reading literature about how persons with traumatic brain injuries act impulsively, and that their instincts might no longer be trustworthy, I found myself constantly fighting my ego, trying to relinquish the control and follow the still, small voice. Since that first *Companions In Christ* study, I had relied on the still, small voice to alert me to God's whispers. I wanted to ensure that I listened not solely to my raw instinct, not solely to my own reason--the two fighting each other, but rather to

God's one voice speaking through both and resolving all dissonance and conflict. Once quiet, I listened and God's promptings became unquestionable. As my self-doubt faded, I discovered opportunities as abundant as the rhizomes.

The announcement inviting artists to submit their work for consideration was from a coffee shop named Heine Brothers which sat across the street from my church. Local and eclectic, Heine Brothers regularly exhibited work by local artists, and it was their announcement I had heard on the radio. I contacted them immediately, before my ego had a chance to plant the seed of doubt. I emailed the manager a photograph of the one piece I had completed and a description of what I thought the final exhibit might look like. Without knowing me or seeing any more art, the manager said *yes*, they were interested in offering me an exhibit slot, but there was a two-year waiting period. Two years might have discouraged some, but a two-year waiting period was perfect for me. It provided a deadline but with enough time to try, fail, try again, fail again, succeed. And two years also gave me time to practice listening to the still, small voice and follow where it led.

Thus, I started to work.

From left to right, the final exhibit comprised, in order: *Plethora; Through a Glass Darkly; Net of Indra; Kaleidoscope Eyes;* and *Abide*. The viewing order for the exhibit was such that the iris reverts from maturity (*Plethora*) to rhizome (*Abide*) and is intended to be viewed from left to right. *Kaleidoscope Eyes, Net of Indra,* and *Through A Glass, Darkly* depict my existence in the years that unfolded as I emerged from coma.

That first painting I produced was from a picture I had taken of that numinous iris in 2007. *Plethora* was the title I decided upon, although loaves and fishes and numinous remained tied for second for many months. In the end, the look and feel of the word plethora was a more illustrative title. Not as literal as loaves and fishes, plethora is graceful and optimistic, and more familiar than numinous.

As I studied my photos of the iris rhizome, it became a metaphor. A rhizome looks like a root or an old, twisted, discarded cigar. It has long, curling tentacles growing from all sides with one or two particularly strong, well-defined roots winding down deep. Whereas invisible in the ground, gradually the rhizome loosened its grip on the emerging flower so that a bright green tip began to push through the surface. Like the rhizome, I had lain waiting, abiding with God, multiple wires connecting me to various machines, and, thankfully, a well-defined connection to the source of my nourishment tethering me to God. To the hospital visitor, I lay in bed without much going on except occasional changes in some numbers on a monitor, but unseen extraordinary changes occurred.

I spent one entire weekend working on *Abide* with unsatisfactory results. In retrospect, the problem was me--again. I was trying to paint my idea rather than listening and abiding in God's grace. I keep that first painting to remind myself what controlling and forcing look like. It differs completely from my finished painting.

The finished piece is longer than it is wide. I cut a recyclable piece of cardboard 20 inches by 60 inches and placed it vertically on my easel. This orientation dedicates as much space to the long roots as it does to the body of the rhizome. I painted the background cream, which gives the rhizome the effect of abiding. The cream color allows a hint of the pattern in the cardboard to be revealed. The honeycomb pattern foreshadows a web referred to in the *Net of Indra*. On the field of cream, I placed the rhizome. Using a 2-inch angled brush loaded with dark brown paint, I lay down the outline of the rhizome and long, curling tendrils trailed below with a few smaller roots extending from the body of the rhizome. Finally, a small bit of green stem begins to sprout from one end reaching upward to penetrate the surface. A visual metaphor, *Abide* is as much a painting about the state of abiding as it is about an emerging iris. This painting I captioned: *Abide-to remain, continue, stay.* Followed by:

> *Under the surface of the earth lay an Iris rhizome. Long roots grew out of the rhizome, absorbing nutrients deep in the ground. Once established, a flower began to emerge. Physically, I was in a coma. My body lay in a bed, still; my spirit was busy, rest-assured. And then I began to emerge.*

I completed what would be the third painting in the exhibit next. The painting I titled *Net of Indra* depicts the interconnectedness defined in the Hindu my *The Jeweled Net of Indra*. I included this caption briefly explaining the myth. The caption reads:

> *The net is a mythical web of precious stones in which each gem reflects all the others, symbolizing the universal connection of everything.*

long as I can remember. This was the dream: It is this web that is partially revealed in *Abide*. We are all connected. This concept was further clarified during the cosmology class I took at Passionist Earth and Spirit Center. My *Net of Indra* painting represents my interpretation of the processing disorder and brain fog I endured. My vision may not have been 20/20 and my response time sluggish, but I settled into that extra time Feldenkrais identified (p. 45) between thought and action, to see. The processing disorder gave me the time.

Through a Glass, Darkly requires some background. During graduate school at the University of Louisville, Donnie and I rented a small house in Elizabethtown, about 45 minutes from the main campus. One morning, when I was about 28, I woke up from a vivid dream and immediately called Sharon to tell her about it. Sharon and I have shared dreams for as

I was below ground in an open, deep hole. People had gathered on the surface, lamenting how sad it was that I had died. "Forty-two is too young to die," someone said. I realized they were talking about me. I wasn't dead even though everyone thought I was. I began clawing my way to the surface, my hands dug into the earth. The hole was my freshly dug grave. The sides had clear shovel marks. "I'm not dead," I shouted. "I'm here. . . I'm here . . . can't you see me? Can't you hear me?"

That one statement--forty-two is too young to die--and the images were so strong that I asked Sharon to remember this for me. I told her that if anything like that ever happened to me, no one would believe I had this dream so I wanted her to be my witness. Some time after my conversation with Sharon, she shared that dream with Mom. Through the years Mom had also shared her vivid, prophetic dreams with us. Mom dreamed she would develop a chronic illness, a cross to bear--she had this dream before being diagnosed with type-one diabetes. She had dreamed Amy would die from leukemia, specifically *leukemia*, two years before Amy's diagnosis. So, Mom was open to the possibility of the prophetic nature of dreams and sensitive to the imagery.

While I was in a coma, Mom and Sharon immediately recognized the correlation between my dream from 15 years earlier and my current condition after the wreck. I was 42 years old.

As I began work on *Through a Glass, Darkly,* my definition of consciousness continued to evolve. It was clear to me that a bas relief communicated much of what I had to say. Part painting, part sculpture, a bas relief was at once two dimensional and three dimensional, projecting from the painting while belonging to the painting. My bas relief would represent action from stillness. Still using the iris as my guiding image, I purchased a frame about five inches deep, 36 inches long and 28" wide. Using the cardboard that accompanied the frame, I sketched out the iris. Next, I began to build the three-dimensional frame on which I would place plaster cloth strips. Once hardened, I painted in the iris.

The final piece produced was, *Kaleidoscope Eyes.* This proved the greatest emotional challenge. As the next to last piece (in exhibit order), it represented the earliest stage of emerging from coma. The lyric from The Beatles song *Lucy In the Sky, with Diamonds* is one I had running in my head for months while in Frasier. I had adopted a clear guiding image from these lyrics: a kaleidoscope. I had a caption to accompany the painting: one I had penned after hearing the length of time a complete recovery could take, but no painting. I had periodically worked on *Kaleidoscope Eyes* but had yet to be confident in the results. Each time I started to paint the piece, the result was too literal. I was holding on too tightly, trying to control the image that represented the exact opposite of control. I was doing the same thing with *Kaleidoscope Eyes* that I had done with *Abide*.

Then, two days before the exhibit opening, I sat down. Reminded myself that any preconceived ideas I had about what the exhibit should be, or how many pieces should be finished, were my own. The artistic expression of returning to this world was inside, I just needed fortitude. I started to paint and, in one sitting, *Kaleidoscope Eyes* was completed. Surrender.

Step Three

At about the same time, I began to formulate a wellness program for active senior adults. As I poured through article after article about rehabilitating my body and my brain a common thread emerged: the "baby boom" generation was retiring and would redefine what it meant to age. "Active aging adult" replaced "senior citizen" and antiquated notions of sterile nursing homes were replaced by retirement communities offering different levels of care. Medical breakthroughs were extending the life expectancy of aging adults, but programs to stimulate the mind and soul were lagging behind. I knew first-hand the skills I had developed through the arts were undeniably a factor in my successful recovery. If I could develop a program to teach those skills to retirees, that population could be better positioned to enjoy the future, rather than endure the future. M*apping the Brain* by Rita Carter was invaluable to me in my understanding of and excitement for research into brain plasticity. The fMRI results documented in that book were like breadcrumbs leading me down a path. And while I accept the limitations of this new research, *it* nevertheless gave me inspiration. I was living a justified life, but not an inspired life, and I missed feeling inspired. I had been inspired to draw and paint, but that was for myself. Could the knowledge I gained in the last 10 years inspire others to fully live the next 10, 20, 30 years of their life?

What first started as a blog about ways seniors could enhance their mental flexibility and mind/body awareness soon turned into an experiential class. With the help of a neurologist and a registered nurse, I documented the results of ten-week training sessions.

The statistics bore out what I hoped. Over a ten-week training period, mental flexibility showed the greatest increase-89%. This kind of intentional training for seniors will change the future for the growing number of aging adults. My recovery is a miracle and one that I believe God presented me with the opportunity to prepare for my entire life. And having prepared, I called on the creative skills I developed when needed. Providing an opportunity to help develop those skills in others, I developed experiential exercises that any one of any age or physical ability could learn and practice. I have included the manual with definitions of important terminology, the ten-week syllabus, and the tools for data collection in the appendix.

So, a ten-piece art exhibit, a wellness class for seniors, and a memoir--my cup overflows.

EPILOGUE

Now you are the body of Christ, and each one of you is a part of it (1 Corinthians 12:27, NIRV). Since Amy's death, I have hoped this teaching from Corinthians was true. Now I know. Knowing that we are all the body of Christ keeps me accountable to all. When we shuffle off this mortal coil we are all the same.

The *Net of Indra* is a metaphor used to illustrate the interconnectedness of everything. This theme is evident throughout God's creation: the fascia that covers our bodies, a thin sheath of fibrous tissue; the microscopic cellular web connecting cell to cell; the vast cosmos, peppered with stars and galaxies whose remnants scientists now believe may eventually find their way into our bodies. John's use of the image of the vine and branches remind us to stay connected to the vine so that the branches will bear good fruit (Jn 15:5, KJV).

As I said, the exhibit was mounted at Heine Bothers coffee shop and then at The Common Cup art gallery at St. Paul United Methodist Church's inaugural opening of the gallery and coffee shop in their family life center. I still enjoy sharing the exhibit through a power point presentation like the one I did for the A.M. Rotary

Club. The fragile nature of *Through A Glass Darkly* currently prevents me from mounting an exhibit, but once I properly anchor that piece I plan to offer it again. *Through A Glass, Darkly* evokes the feeling of emerging from the canvas and continuing through the glass of the frame. I plan to use a technique called "slumping". This technique would allow me to sculpt the glass to reflect the iris as it breaks through into our world; like the iris, my emergence was a gift from God, and cannot be contained.

Donnie and I just celebrated our 32nd wedding anniversary. Mom continues to inspire me, and Sharon works as a nurse for The Norfolk Naval Hospital. Audrey graduated The University of Kentucky and Logan is a freshman at U. K.

So, in 2010 as I spoke to that Rotary Club, I couldn't imagine it would be more than five years before I started to put in to words something resembling my experience. The experience remains as palpable today as in 2004.

White Noise is the title of my next painting in the exhibit. *IN* and *OUT* represent going in to and out of that ineffable place. With paint and canvas, I hope to explore what is there less literally, pray I may be given eyes to see, and again, listen. I will probably spend the rest of my time on earth trying to explain what I experienced in the coma, but searching for God in every day occurrences is a pretty good way to spend my time. As Merton said, "I hope that I will never do anything apart from that desire to please You."

The still, small voice in you is whispering to you. You may choose to dismiss its relevance, which is of course your prerogative. Or define it as secular rather than sacred, keeping your intuition grounded and small, in a frame with clearly defined perimeters. Or, you can give what I believe a try: the still, small voice is God breaking through my busyness and ego, speaking to me, through me. I need only listen. And as I listen, I am reminded that I am not alone.

I will not leave you comfortless: I will come to you. Yet a little while, and the world seeth me no more; but ye see me: because I live, ye shall live also. (Jn 14:18-19. KJV)

The Irises 2012

Part Two

Learning H.O.W. to Age™

Wellness Program

Introduction

Expressive Avenues: Wellness philosophy is one of intentional practice, encouraging mental curiosity and improving the quality of life. The National Wellness Institute defines seven dimensions of wellness; emotional, occupational, physical, social, intellectual, spiritual and environmental. Of those seven, only physical wellness is consistently part of a wellness practice. Physical wellness has become a well-documented and soughtafter goal for many years. After all, there are very specific metrics for measuring physical wellness and years of statistics to back up claims. As a society, we have learned that a healthy body has a positive influence on things like blood pressure, heart disease, joint fluidity and mood. Having reaped the rewards of physical wellness, doesn't it make sense to attack the other aspects of wellness with the same enthusiasm? But how are the other aspects of wellness addressed and tested? What are the *goals* and benefits?

As we retire from the work force we are at risk from a sedentary lifestyle; however, only the physical body (weight, muscle mass, blood pressure, etc.) have been targeted--until now.

Recent discoveries support that the mental, social, spiritual and emotional life of someone retired and aging needs as much attention and focus as the physical body. Through advances in brain mapping, researchers have shown a correlation between a particular activity and increased energy activity in the region of the brain associated with that activity. Preventing age related accidents due to loss of balance, and encouraging social interaction and critical decision-making may be a matter of igniting the release of neurotransmitters in the region of the brain associated with these skills.

In 2012, Expressive Avenues: Wellness documented participants engaged in Learning H.O.W. to Age ™ for ten weeks. The target participants for

Learning H.O.W. to Age™ (abbreviated to L.H.T.A.) are retirees, 65 years old and older, and in good general health. Each lesson in this program was developed with a specific goal in mind and tested on aging adults living independently in a retirement community. L.H.T.A. focused on the previously mentioned dimensions of wellness not typically addressed: intellectual, occupational, social, environmental, emotional and spiritual wellness. Each of these exercises are rooted in documented scientific studies and validated by leading thinkers in the fields of neurology, psychology, physics and kinesiology.

Based on fMRI brain mapping results illustrated in Mapping the Mind by Rita Carter and referencing Moshe Feldenkrais, Abraham Maslow, Edward de Bono and Dr. Richard Restak, Expressive Avenues: Wellness synthesized their theories and philosophies and combined them with experiential gaming and awareness exercises used in acting, dance and voice. The psycho-social wellness program, Learning H.O.W. to Age™, is the result. In addition, Expressive Avenues: Wellness developed a toolkit for collecting and analyzing data related to this wellness program. The scientific and medical community supports the continued development of the skills practiced in L.H.T.A. and has determined those skills as crucial to a successful retirement free of anxiety, illness, and social isolation.

Learning H.O.W. to Age™ was developed in response to the growing population of retirees, the escalating costs of medical care and the general decline in quality of life seen in this population. The validity of this program lies not only in the immediate results but in the long-term wellness benefits. Joining these particular acting and movement exercises with accepted therapeutic outcomes offers participants the promise of vibrant living throughout a lifetime.

The Program

This program includes: a ten-week participatory class with weekly lessons, exercises, and tools for charting progress and monitoring growth. Instructions assume a facilitator; however, exercises are adaptable and a *participant* can step out of the role of participant and into the role of facilitator as needed.

Each lesson explains the exercise and skill developed or enhanced and the scoring rubric for that exercise. Space for further exercise development, suggested topics for group discussion, and journal responses is also provided.

Exercises are intended to be interwoven. The skill you develop in one exercise will be reinforced in another. Because exercises will be combined to increase skill level, the lessons are numbered numerically with the first number indicating the lesson number and the second number indicating the next exercise in the series. For instance: 2.6 is the second lesson and the sixth exercise in the program. Exercise six may be revisited in the ninth lesson with some increased challenge, and is indicated as 9.6 (ninth lesson and sixth exercise). A numerical list of exercise is included.

Exercises are most effective in groups of six or more. Suggestions for developing a group include: having a predetermined amount of time at the beginning of class to openly discuss a focused question; using the warm-up exercises at the beginning of each meeting; reminding participants to speak from their own experiences only, as social interaction, community building, and trust among group participants is essential. Measured responses blunt creativity and limit potential. Trust allows for a free exchange of ideas and expression. Self-conscious behavior must recede, allowing for authentic expression. The desire to "get it right" is a hurdle no matter the age and must be cleared as soon as possible to allow for the most benefit. Keeping the goal of the exercise foremost in mind will alleviate this tendency. Whenever possible, *focus* your attention on attaining the goal of the exercise instead of yourself.

Modifications are made as needed keeping in mind the goal of an exercise rather than the execution of individual steps. For example, the Moving Meditation exercise includes bilateral arm movements reaching overhead. One group member was unable to lift arms overhead. Rather than abandon the entire exercise, the execution of that particular part was modified for that participant.

It is important to master one level of an exercise before increasing the *cognitive load*. Skills which become habitual free up mental energy making it more possible to accept new information successfully.

It is recommended that you have a doctor's o.k. before engaging in LHTA. LHTA should challenge you mentally and physically; however, you know your capabilities and should rely on your own judgment when mastering these skills.

A definition of italicized words is found in the glossary. Equipment needed for this program is limited to a 12-14 play ball readily accessible at most food or drug stores. A demonstration of the Coordination/Flow and Moving Meditation exercises is available on You

Tube by entering Expressive Avenues Wellness in the search. A blank journal is recommended.

Special Thanks

To Jim Tompkins for sharing his creative gifts, for keeping the bar high and for his friendship. To residents of The Village at Wesley Manor in Louisville Kentucky for their willingness to explore the multifaceted dimensions of wellness. To Norma Henderson for her commitment to her residents and to Charles Hubscher, Phd. and Sharon Darrell, R.N. for their assistance and analysis in developing assessment and data collection guidelines.

Assessment

Mental Flexibility

- Participants stand or sit in a circle in a *neutral position*.
- Exercise is silent.
- Participants toss and catch a 12 to 14-inch ball without a break in rhythm.
- If no facilitator, the group designates a participant to begin and end the exercise.
- If additional challenge added, specify here _____

Skills Assessed

- *mental flexibility*
- *interdependence*

A predetermined alert may be as simple as the facilitator's calling "stop" after an agreed time.

Participant Log- Mental Flexibility--Ball Toss

Name	Date	Point value 1st assessment	Point value 2nd assessment	%Difference

Skill Level	Specification	Point Value
Essential	Continually toss and catch the ball	1 point
Adequate	Continually toss and catch while maintaining silence	2 points

Skill Level	Specification	Point Value
Proficient	Continually toss and catch, maintain silence, hold neutral position	3 points
Superior	Continually toss and catch, maintain silence, hold neutral position, concentrate on activity while increasing tempo	4 points
Excellent	Continually toss and catch, maintain silence, hold neutral position, concentrate on activity while increasing tempo until a predetermined alert signifies completion of exercise	5 points

Physical Perception

- Measure a distance of 15 feet or more.
- Mark beginning point A and ending point B.

- Participant estimates the number of steps from point A to point B.
- *Facilitator* counts the number of steps actually taken as participant increases cognitive load (CL) by repeating aloud a known passage or performing mental math calculations while walking.
- Compare participant's estimated number of steps to facilitator's count of actual steps. Difference between estimate and actual determines skill level.

- If additional challenge added, specify here
  _____

Skills Assessed
- Awareness of external environment
- *Structural integrity*

Participant Log Physical Perception

Participants Name	DATE	DISTANCE	Est.	Actual	% Diff.

Participants Name	DATE	DISTANCE	Est.	Actual	% Diff.

Skill Level	Specifications	Point Value
Essential	Estimated number of steps from point A to point B is 20% of actual number of steps	1 point
Adequate	Estimated number of steps from point A to point B is between 20% and 40% of actual number of steps and *gaze* remains on point B	2 points
Proficient	Estimated number of steps from point A to point B is between 40% and 60% of actual number of steps, gaze remains on point B, and gait is steady	3 points
Superior	Estimated number of steps from point A to point B is between 60% and 80% of actual number of steps, gaze remains on point B, and gait is steady	4 points

Skill Level	Specifications	Point Value
Excellent	Estimated number of steps from point A to point B is between 80% and 100% of actual number of steps, gaze remains on point B, and gait is steady	5 points

Kinesthetic Awareness

- Participants stand or sit in a neutral position.
- Each raise both arms above head, palms facing in.
- Count 1: participant's right shoulder rotates forward, lowering extended arm to the side, palm facing down.
- Count 2: participant's arm movement continues counterclockwise as right arm bends at elbow and palm passes chin, hand rotates turning palm to right ear.
- Count 3: participant's right arm extends up, returning to starting position.

- Left arm mirrors movement, but begins after right arm reaches count 1.

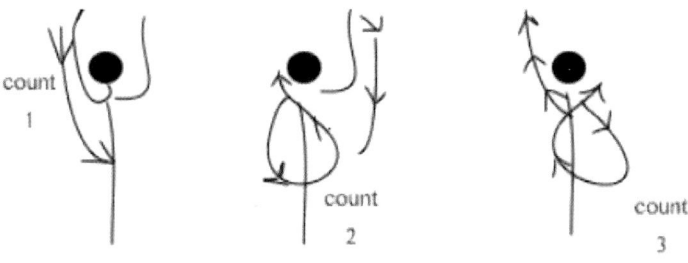

- If additional challenge added, specify here
  _____

Skills Assessed

- *Coordination*
- Flow
- Crossing *midline*

Participant Log

Participant Name	Date	Point value 1st Assessment	Point value 2nd Assessment	% Difference

Participant Name	Date	Point value 1st Assessment	Point value 2nd Assessment	% Differe

Skill Level	Specifications	Point Value	
Essential	Arms move in unison	1 point	
Adequate	Arms move in unison for 3 distinct moves	2 points	
Proficient	Arms alternate movement for 3 distinct moves	3 points	
Superior	Arms alternate movement for 3 distinct moves, and flow is continuous	4 points	
Excellent	Arms alternate movement for 3 distinct moves, flow is continuous, and specific direction	5 points	

Skill Level	Specifications	Point Value	
	of the palm is correct		

If all participants achieve excellent in mental flexibility or individually for physical perception and/or *kinesthetic awareness*, the facilitator should increase the cognitive load. Additional challenges can be found in Appendix B.

Lessons

One

1.1. Warm up:

memory. The goal is to recall all information in the order it was given.

- Begin in a circle, standing or sitting in a neutral position.
- A participant speaks their name and a one-word occupation ("Janice, teacher").
- Moving right, the next participant repeats the first person's name and occupation, then states their own name and occupation.
- Continuing right, the third participant repeats the first and second participants information, and adds their own name and occupation. This pattern continues until each person in the circle has added their name and occupation.

Skills Developed/Enhanced: *working memory*, vocal strength, discipline

GRADE	
A	Able to recall 100% of the information
B	Able to recall 80% of the information
C	Able to recall 50% of the information
D	Able to recall 20% of the information

Grade: _____

Group Discussion: Was the group successful? Within the given parameters, what changes can be made to facilitate success?

Journal Response: Were you successful at recalling information? If you had difficulty, were you able to stay engaged in the activity (eyes focused on the speaker, standing or sitting in a neutral position, focus on the goal, etc.). Notes:

1.2 Gaze:

The goal is to determine habitual gaze and its impact on *gate*. Structural integrity refers to holding the body in proper alignment allowing the skeleton to support the body with ease. The level at which a person's gaze habitually falls effects the rest of their body. Therefore, addressing habitual gaze quickly corrects posture and strengthen muscles, ligaments and tendons. If no facilitator, work in pairs.

- Participant selects an object 10-15' away (a picture on a wall, a window, etc.). If imagined, object should be imagined at eye level.
- Participant focuses on this object (what does it look like: color, texture, weight, etc.).
- Participant closes their eyes and creates a mental image of the distance between themselves and the object.
- Participant estimates how many steps it will take them to reach the object.

- Participant opens their eyes.
- Facilitator records participant's estimate.
- Participant walks to object, speaking aloud a memorized passage or mathematical calculation.
- Facilitator counts and records the number of steps actually taken.
- Compare the estimated steps to the actual number of steps taken.
- Record your results.

Skills Developed/Enhanced: kinesthetic awareness, physical perception and structural integrity.

Journal Response: How interesting was the object? How important to you? If imagined, were you able to hold the image in your mind while reciting the passage aloud? How easy or difficult did you find it to maintain your gaze? What effect did this have on your gate? You may feel taller, larger, and more confident. In what way did this exercise change your visual perspective? How can the effects of this exercise transfer to your daily life?

In what way? As you expand your awareness, what precautions might you take to safe guard against balance issues or "stubbing" your toe? As the level of gaze improves so does structural integrity and awareness of environment. Notes:

1.3: Ball Toss:

The goal is to keep the ball in play.
- Begin in a circle, standing or sitting in a neutral position.
- Toss the ball around the circle continuously.
- Exercise is silent.

Once the goal is achieved consistently, increase the cognitive load by adding a commonly known, memorized passage (Pledge of Allegiance, Mary Had a Little Lamb, etc.).

- Decide if passage is to be divided by word or phrase.
- Toss the ball and speak one word or phrase when the ball is tossed. This pattern continues, until the entire passage is spoken in sequence or the ball is dropped.
- Limit your speaking to the passage.
- Next, say the word or phrase when catching the ball and compare any difference. Abdominal muscles automatically engage when tossing the ball. Speaking when you toss the ball encourages proper breath support for your voice, and often results in stronger, clearer *intonation*.

Skills Developed/Enhanced: mental flexibility, interdependence, physical perception, group goal achievement, social interaction and camaraderie.

Group Discussion: Does increasing cognitive load compliment or detract from the primary goal? How can the two be integrated? Did the agreed upon text sound conversational or robotic? Why or why not?

Journal response: When the exercise was silent, were you successful using visual cues only? Why or why not? How did your breathing change? Notes:

Two

2.1 Warm up:

Memory. Participants specify a personal goal in addition to the group goal of the warm up.

- Begin in a circle, standing or sitting in a neutral position.
- A participant speaks their name and a one-word occupation ("Janice, teacher").

- Moving right, the next participant repeats the first person's name and occupation, then states their own name and occupation.
- Continuing right, the third participant repeats the first and second participants information, and adds their own name and occupation. This pattern continues until each person in the circle has added their name and occupation.

Skills Developed/Enhanced: strengthen working memory, vocal strength, discipline, camaraderie, establishing a personal goal which supports the group goal.

Group Discussion: Was the group successful or unsuccessful? Why or why not?

Journal Response: "When the exercise was silent, were you successful using visual cues only? Why or why not? How did your breathing change? Notes:

2.4 Coordination/Flow/Guiding Image:

The goal of the exercise is to move in a coordinated and fluid manner. The addition of a *guiding image* is introduced to connect the physical movement with a mental image.

- Participants stand or sit in a neutral position.
- Raise both arms above head, palms facing in.
- Count 1: participant's right shoulder rotates forward, lowering extended arm to the side, palm facing down.
- Count 2: participant's arm movement continues counterclockwise as right arm bends at elbow and palm passes chin, hand rotates turning palm to right ear.
- Count 3: participant's right arm extends up, returning to starting position.

- Left arm mirrors movement, but begins after right arm reaches count 1.

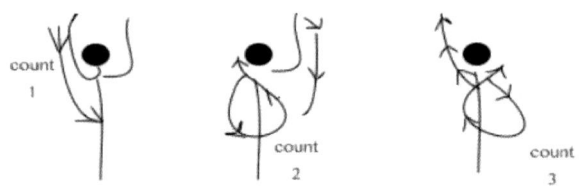

- Repeat movement pattern with eyes closed. If balance is a challenge, a piece of furniture touching the backs of legs offers assurance. Feel it against your legs. Chin remains level, spine lengthens.
- As the movement becomes fluid and connected, allow images to guide the movement.

Skills Developed/Enhanced: *crossing the mid-line*, coordination, fluidity. Increasing sensitivity to movement, mental discipline.

Journal Response: Did you maintain structural integrity throughout? Were you able to "sense" the physical movement rather than "watch"? Fine tuning sensation within yourself is necessary to strengthen kinesthetic awareness. Feel the sole of the foot in your shoe against the floor. This intentional focus will ground you and may alleviate the feeling of a loss of balance. Did the addition of a guiding image help the execution of the movement? Elaborate. What did you notice about your breathing? Your structural integrity? Inefficient muscle tension? If the chosen image does not help, continue to develop one that does. Suggestions are: a fountain, pulling taffy, a rubber band, etc. Notes:

2.5 Moving Meditation:

The goal is to build physical flexibility and mental duration.

- Move a stable chair to an open space and use the chair as needed for balance.

- Special attention should be paid to alignment, proper joint rotation and abdominals.
- Once learned, this pattern repeats four times to the right immediately followed by four times to the left.
- Exercise should be guided by a facilitator prepared to work through the exercise and lead the class.

Count	Movement
one	arms vertical, palms in
two	eyes look up, chin remains level
three, four	sweep arms back, around, bend knees
five	bend elbows, palms up, eyes lower to look at palms
six	straighten knees to stand, hands close to fists, elbows move back moving fists to waist, eyes forward
seven	step R forward to lunge, extend both arms forward, palms up
eight	step L to meet R both legs straight, open arms out, palms forward
nine	step R out, R arm down, L arm up
ten	flex R foot to lift toes and rotate hip open to point toes R, bend elbow, lower L arm
eleven	bend R knee, R arm extends, head turns R

Count	Movement
twelve	L arm bends, at elbow, L heel raise and L knee bends rotating L hip under to re-align hips
thirteen	step L to R, straighten knees to standing, extend L arm forward, palms up

Skills Developed/Enhanced: *Physical perception*, kinesthetic awareness, structural integrity, *core strength*, balance, working memory. **Journal Response:** Besides working on the physical pattern, what other ways might you work on this? What do you feel or see? What images, abstract or otherwise, come to mind? Notes:

Three

3.1 Warm up: Memory.

The goal is development of strategies for improving memory. Participants specify a personal goal in addition to the group goal.

- Begin in a circle, standing or sitting in a neutral position.
- Participant speaks a sequence of 3 words.
- In turn, the next participant on the right repeats the first person's sequence, then states their own sequence.
- Continuing right, the third participant repeats the first and second participants information, and adds their own sequence. This pattern continues until each participant in the circle has added their sequence.

Skills Developed/Enhanced: strengthen working memory, vocal strength, discipline, camaraderie, developing strategies for success.

Group Discussion: Was the group successful or unsuccessful? Why or why not?

Journal Response: Indicate your personal goal and its effect. Give yourself a grade

Grade: _____

A   Able to recall 100% of the information
B   Able to recall 80% of the information
C   Able to recall 50% of the information
D   Able to recall 20% of the information

Notes:

Review briefly Coordination/Flow

3.6 Moving Meditation: Detail

Facilitator works through each count establishing proper alignment.

1. "Stand with feet shoulder width apart with toes pointing forward. Arms rise forward with palms of

hands facing in. Arms continue to rise overhead with finger tips pointing up."

2. "Eye balls roll up in sockets to look at fingers. The neck is only engaged if necessary and participants focus should be on lifting the chin and stretching the front of the neck as opposed to contracting the back of the neck."

3. "Bend knees, arms sweep back and down, eyes continue looking up."

4. "Elbows bend at the waist, palms of hands face up."

5. "Eyes lower to look at hands."

6. "Knees straighten, eyes look forward, hands close to fists and arms move back, parallel to ground."

7. "Right leg steps forward with knee bent and left foot lifting onto the ball of the foot. Arms extend forward, hands open with palms up."

8. "Left foot joins the right, palms rotate forward as arms open."

9. "Right foot steps to right with toes remaining forward, right arm lowers to side as left arm raises."

10. "Right foot flexes shifting weight to the heel. Right arm moves counter-clockwise as left arm sweeps clockwise."

11. "Arms continue moving like the hands of a clock as right hip rotates out, left foot lifts the heel and pushes to the ball of the foot, and torso realigns 1/4 turn to the right."

12. "Right elbow bends, right forearm continues across body and behind the left arm. Left arm continues clockwise sweep. Right arm extends straight with palm up, and left elbow bends at the waist with palm up. Weight shifts to front foot and torso aligns."

13 "Left foot joins right, left arm extends straight with palm up."

3.7 Breathing Basics

CAUTION: Light-headedness is common when practicing *diaphragmatic breathing*. Remaining seated is necessary for safety.

When you sleep or physically exert yourself, when your pet breathes or a baby cries, the *diaphragm* expands and contracts naturally. Intentionally focusing on this breathing pattern keeps your body and brain flooded with oxygen, encourages flexibility in your lungs and provides your voice with the support needed to speak clearly. If this approach to intentional diaphragmatic breathing remains difficult, try lying on your back in bed before you rise, and placing a hand between your bellybutton and ribs. Relax your shoulders and pay attention to your breath in this position.

This exercise is designed to draw your awareness to your body's natural breathing pattern. Avoid any artificial manipulation. The goal is to locate and intentionally breathe from your diaphragm.

- In a seated neutral position, place one hand on the chest and other hand on abdomen under ribcage and above belly button.
- Relax abdominal muscles
- Inhale and exhale, paying attention to any physical movement.
- The hand on the chest should stay still as the hand on the abdomen moves forward and back laterally.
- Next, using a feather or slip of paper, hold the object in one hand, extend the arm in front.
- Imagine the object is a candle or match. In one explosive breath, blow out the flame. Repeat 3-5 times.

Skills Developed/Enhanced: *Mind/body connection*, mental focus, diaphragmatic control.

Journal Response: Did an image aid in locating the diaphragm? When can this kind of breathing be incorporated in your life? Notes:

Four

4.3 Warm Up: Ball Toss

- The goal of the exercise is to keep the ball in play.

- Before beginning, the group must decide the following:
    1. passage to be spoken
    2. division of the passage by word or phrase

- Speaking will occur when tossing the ball.

- Exercise is silent unless speaking next word or phrase in the passage.

- If the ball is dropped, or passage forgotten, the group begins again.

- A page of additional challenges can be found after the glossary.

4.8 *Blocking*

Blocking is the term used describe the precise movement of actors on stage. Using the areas of the stage illustrated below, participants will learn to fine tune spatial awareness and physical perception by grounding themselves in a universal layout which can be applied to any locale. Stage direction is from the perspective of the actor looking out to the audience, in this case the perspective of the participant. The goal is to familiarize participants with the areas of a stage.

- Designate a specific space with determined parameters. Set this up as the exercise area.

- Facilitator directs participants to specific areas.

Audience

~~stage Left~~	Downstage	Downstage Right
Centerstage Left	Centerstage	Centerstage Right
Upstage Left	Upstage	Upstage Right

Backstage

4.9 Moving Through The Space

**CAUTION If you are dizzy or feel unstable with eyes closed, when the facilitator says "Stop", position yourself by a chair or table. Allowing a stationary object to come in contact with your body when eyes are closed helps alleviate insecurity or dizziness. The goal is to recognize kinesthetic awareness.

Facilitator instructs participants to:

- "Begin to walk freely within the parameters." Approximately 20 seconds.
- "Stop (standing or sitting) in a neutral position. Close your eyes." **
- "Focus on internal awareness and momentarily place a hand on the area where you feel your presence." 20-30 seconds.
- "Release your hand to your side. Open your eyes and walk through the space again, slow your pace and shorten your stride." 20 seconds.

- Repeat steps 2 and 3
- "Open your eyes and walk through the space with a comfortable stride."
- "Slow your pace and lengthen your stride."
- Repeat steps 2 and 3. Make a mental note of any difference.
- "Open your eyes and begin to walk through the space with a comfortable stride. Now alter your pace and stride to your preference."
- "Stop (standing or sitting) in a neutral position. Close your eyes." ** Place a hand on the area where you feel your presence." 20-30 seconds.

Skills Developed/Enhanced: kinesthetic awareness.

Journal Response: Was it easy or difficult to locate the area in your body where you feel present? When eyes were open, where did your gaze rest? Did gaze change when you changed your stride? How? What unnecessary muscle tension did you have? Notes:

Five

<u>Recall Development</u>

Functional MRI (magnetic resonance imaging), is making it possible to correlate specific activities with specific regions of the brain. Consequently, when those same activities are recalled, those same areas of the brain show engagement. Sense memory or sensory recall has been utilized as an acting method for many years. Dr. Richard Restak, author and Clinical Professor of Neurology at The George Washington School of Medicine and Health Science cites a common acting exercise in which novice actors are taught to use their sense memory as a plasticity-enhancing exercise for the brain. Let me stress that the success of sense memory relies on the details recalled. A general recollection (the taste of a medium-well filet mignon is delicious) is not enough to ignite neurological responses. But, learning and practicing detailed recall (the taste, texture, temperature, weight etc.) can result in neurological activity similar to the real event.

5.6 Warm up: Moving Meditation

Count	Movement
one	arms vertical, palms in
two	eyes look up, chin remains level
three, four	sweep arms back, around, bend knees
five	bend elbows, palms up, eyes lower to look at pa
six	straighten knees to stand, hands close to fists, elbows move back moving fists to waist, eyes forward
seven	step R forward to lunge, extend both arms forw palms up
eight	step L to meet R both legs straight, open arms o palms forward
nine	step R out, R arm down, L arm up
ten	flex R foot to lift toes and rotate hip open to poi toes R, bend R elbow, lower L arm
eleven	bend R knee, R arm extends, head turns R
twelve	L arm bends, at elbow, L heel raise and L knee bends rotating L hip under to re-align hips
thirteen	step L to R, straighten knees to standing, extend arm forward, palms up

5.10 Sensory Recall:

The goal is to recall, in as much detail as possible, past experiences.

1. In pairs, take turns describing for each other a savory dish or food. Recall not only tastes and smells but location, presentation of the dish, ambient sounds, temperature of the dish and of the feel of the atmosphere, emotional responses, etc.

Journal Response: Notes

2. In pairs, take turns describing for each other a happy occasion. Describe who, what, when, where, and why. What happens to your breathing? To the pitch and volume of your voice.

Journal Response: When listening to your partner, what do you hear and see? Look at their eyes, what do you notice? Notes

Skills Developed/Enhanced: Accuracy in recall, multi-sensory involvement

5.11 Add on Group Improvisation

Improvisation requires mental flexibility. Like sense recall, *improvisation* is a skill actors work to develop, and so improvisation is included in this program. The goal is to respond in a realistic way to imagined circumstances.

- For the purposes of this program, all improvisation should be based in reality.

- Existing objects are used to define a locale. For example: a desk and chairs are used to establish a kitchen with table and chairs, another desk represents the sink.

- Objects may represent something different from what the object actually is, if that object is defined before the action begins.

- A facilitator starts and stops the improvisation.

- A participant begins the scenario by recreating an activity that would naturally occur.

- After a minute or two, another participant joins the improvisation adding another activity naturally occurring.

- After a minute or two, another participant joins the scenario and this continues until everyone has added something OR the scenario comes to a natural conclusion. For example:

The scenario is a grocery store. The first participant pantomimes stocking the shelves. After the activity has been established, another participant "adds on" a cashier scanning merchandise, a third participant becomes the customer unloading the contents of a cart onto the conveyor belt for the cashier to scan. Another participant adds to the improvisation by acting out a customer with a cart going down the aisle where the stock person is stocking shelves and asks, "Excuse me, can you tell me where spaghetti sauce is?", and so on. As each participant joins the improvisation, details become fleshed out and a scene takes shape.

- Participants continue to "add-on" to the scene until the facilitator calls "stop".
- "Stop" may be called if:

    1. The scene is going well and comes to a natural conclusion. If this is the case, end the scene and begin another.

    2. No one engages with the first volunteer. If this is the case, end the scene and establish one or two details to jump-start the improvisation.

3. Participation has halted with several other options still available. If this is the case, end the scene and ask what other options have yet to be addressed?

Skills Developed/Enhanced: mental flexibility, spatial awareness, recall, imagination

Group Discussion: How much time did the group take to fully develop a scenario? When the improvisation stopped, were there other details to be added? What is the story of this scenario? Based on knowledge from the lesson devoted to blocking, sketch a layout of the scenario that was unfolding. Does your layout match the others?

Journal Response: Did you join in this improvisation? Why or why not? Did you listen to the improvisation and allow the activity to create a mental image or were you thinking of an activity that you could add in? If another participant added in an activity that you were planning to add, were you able think of something different? Notes:

If you seem unable to think of something to do, it is possible you are limiting your flow of ideas by placing your attention on yourself and the stress that induces, rather than paying attention to the scene. Examine whether or not your attention is on your self or on the scenario. Moving your attention outside of your self and onto the scenario often helps to lift this barrier allowing a freer flow of ideas or brainstorming to occur. This encourages mental flexibility. Notes:

Six

6.6 Warm up: Moving Meditation

6.12 Imagination Development:

Story-A-Round with ball toss

- The goal of this exercise is to create a story with a beginning, middle, simultaneously keeping the ball in play.
- Participants are limited to two sentences or phrases.
- Standing or sitting in a circle, one participant starts a story and tosses the ball.
- The participant who catches the ball adds to the story with a sentence or phrase that further develops the story as they toss the ball.
- The creation of the story must follow the guidelines of the world in which this story exists, not necessarily the guidelines of the rational world in which we live.
- The exercise continues until facilitator calls "Stop".

If the story begins to fall along the lines of a well-known story (Goldilocks and the Three Bears for example), stop the exercise and begin again. Encourage the participants to allow their own imagination to write the story, allowing any visual images to evoke actions and character. They will find the more engaged they become in creating the story, the more impact the story will have on their enjoyment of the exercise and their memory of the story.

Skills Developed/Enhanced: intentional focus, listening, working memory, *general memory*, imagination

Group discussion: How successful was the group at creating a story? Why or why not? Did each addition make sense to the existing narrative? What restrictions did the group assume? Were these restrictions helpful in achieving the goal?

Journal Response: What, if anything, prevented you from fully participating in this exercise? What might your willingness or unwillingness to fully take part tell you about your presence in your daily life activities? Notes:

6.13 Mirror

- The goal is to create the image of a reflection.
- A facilitator is preferred.
- The exercise is silent.
- Each pair designates one leader and one mirror.
- In pairs, either seated or standing, establish eye contact and maintain eye contact throughout the exercise.
- Once eye contact is established, a facilitator begins calling "Start".
- The leader moves and the mirror reflects back the movements.
- After minute or two, facilitator switches the roles of the leader and the reflection.

Skills Developed/Enhanced: physical perception, *expanding awareness*

Journal Response: Were you able to maintain your focus on the goal? How, if at all, did the movement change? Were you able to maintain structural integrity throughout the exercise? While maintaining eye contact, how did your awareness of your environment change? How might you continue to develop this expanded awareness in your daily activities? Notes:

Seven

7.5 Warm up:

Coordination/Flow + Guiding Image-

- Guiding Image_____ If no specific image comes to mind use a cascading fountain.

7.14 Introduction to Awareness Through Movement and *Moshe Feldenkrais*

Moshe Feldenkrais was a thought leader and advocates for the connection between thought and its effect on movement. Now, fMRI results are proving him correct. Most importantly, that connection can be felt in the practitioners. The delay between thought and action is the basis for awareness (Feldenkrais, Moshé. Awareness through Movement: Easy-to-do Health Exercises to Improve Your Posture, Vision, Imagination, and Personal Awareness. New York City: HarperCollins, 1990. Print. p.60) and this delay allows for correction of inefficient or harmful movement. Developing an awareness of functional movement is a primary goal. Incorporating that awareness into daily activity results in a stronger mind and body. The *Feldenkrais Method* uses small, repetitive physical movements, combined with mental recall of the movement, to teach awareness of physical movement and correct habitual inefficient movement patterns.

Participants sit with enough space between chairs to rise and move.
    1. Relax jaw with lips together.
        a. clinch and relax jaw. Repeat 25 times
        b. recall the exercise mentally by closing eyes and recalling the sensations felt
    2. Relax tongue and rest the tongue behind teeth.
        a. raise tongue to the roof of your mouth then relax. Repeat 25 times
        b. recall mentally by closing eyes and recalling sensations
    3. The *dynamic* link between standing and sitting. (Feldenkrais 78-82).

The unnecessary tension created when clinching the jaw or holding the tongue to the roof of the mouth is one example of myriad pockets of unnecessary tension we carry daily. "Superfluous efforts shorten (contract) the body" (Feldenkrais. 96) and may be eliminated with practice. "It is impossible to change habit by sensation alone. Some conscious mental effort must be made until the adjusted position ceases to feel abnormal and becomes the new habit." (Feldenkrais, p.60).

Eight

8.12 Warm Up: Story-A-Round with ball toss

- The goal of this exercise is to create a story with a beginning, middle, and end while keeping the ball in play.
- Participants are limited to two sentences or phrases.
- In a circle, one participant begins a story and tosses the ball.
- The participant who catches the ball adds to the story with a sentence or phrase that develops the story as they toss the ball.

- The creation of the story must follow the guidelines of the world in which this story exists, not necessarily the guidelines of the rational world in which we live.
- The exercise continues until a facilitator calls "Stop".

If the story begins to fall along the lines of a well-known story (Goldilocks and the Three Bears for example), stop the exercise and begin again. Encourage the participants to allow their own imagination to write the story, allowing any visual images to evoke actions and character. They will find that the more active and engaged they are in the creation of the story, the more interesting the story.

Skills Developed/Enhanced: intentional focus, listening, working memory, general memory, imagination

Group discussion: How successful was the group at creating a story? Why or why not? Did each addition make sense to the existing narrative? What restrictions did the group place on themselves? Were these restrictions helpful in achieving the goal?

Journal Response: What, if anything, prevented you from fully participating in this exercise? What might your willingness or unwillingness to fully participate tell you about your presence in your daily life activities? Notes:

8.11 Add-On Group Improvisation

Improvisation requires mental flexibility. Like sense recall, improvisation is a skill actors work to develop, and so improvisation is included in this program.

- The goal is to respond in a realistic way to imagined circumstances
- For the purposes of this program, all improvisation should be based in reality

- Existing objects should be used to aid in defining a locale
- Objects may represent something different from what the object is, if that object is defined before the action begins
- A facilitator starts and stops the improvisation.
- A participant begins the scenario by creating activity that would naturally occur
- After a minute or two, another participant joins the improvisation adding another activity naturally occurring.
- After a minute or two, another participant joins the improvisation adding another activity naturally occurring.
- After a minute or two, another participant joins the scenario and this continues until everyone has added something OR the scenario comes to a natural conclusion.

8.6 Moving Meditation: Detail

Facilitator works through each count establishing proper alignment.

    1. "Stand feet shoulder width apart with toes pointing forward. Arms rise forward with palms of hands facing in. Arms continue to rise overhead with finger tips pointing up."

    2. "Eye balls roll up in sockets to look at fingers." The neck is only engaged if necessary and the participants focus should be on lifting the chin and stretching the front of the neck as opposed to contracting the back of the neck.

    3. "As knees begin to bend, arms sweep back and down, eyes remain looking up."

    4. "Elbows bend at the waist, palms of hands face up."

    5. "Eyes lower to look at hands."

6. "Knees straighten, eyes look forward, hands close to fists and arms move back, parallel to ground."

7. "Right leg steps forward with knee bent, left heel lifts up shifting body weight onto the ball of the foot. Arms extend forward, hands open with palms up."

8. "Left foot joins the right, palms rotate forward as arms open."

9. "Right foot steps to right with toes remaining forward, right arm lowers to side as left arm raises."

10. "Right foot flexes shifting weight to the heel. Right arm moves counter-clockwise as left arm sweeps clockwise."

11. "Arms continue moving like the hands of a clock as right hip rotates out, left foot lifts the heel and pushes to the ball of the foot, and torso realigns 1/4 turn to the right."

12. "Right elbow bends, right forearm continues across body and behind the left arm. Left arm continues clockwise sweep. Right arm extends straight with palm up, and left elbow bends waist with palm up. Weight has shifted to front foot and torso is aligned."

13 "Left foot joins right, left arm extends straight with palm up."

Nine

9.13 Warm Up: Mirror

- The goal of this exercise is to create the image of a mirror reflection.
- A facilitator is preferred.
- The exercise is silent.
- Each pair designates one leader and one mirror.
- In pairs, either seated or standing, establish eye contact and maintain eye contact throughout the exercise.

- When eye contact is established, a facilitator signals to begin.
- The leader begins to move and the mirror reflects back the movements.
- After a few minutes, a facilitator switches the roles of the leader and the mirror.

Skills Developed/Enhanced: physical perception, expanding awareness

Journal Response: Were you able to maintain your focus on the goal? How, if at all, did the movement change? Were you able to maintain structural integrity throughout the exercise? While maintaining eye contact, how did your awareness of your environment change? How might you continue to develop this expanded awareness in your daily activities? Notes:

9.5 Coordination/Flow + Guiding Image

- Exercise goal is to connect the movement fluidly with eyes closed focusing on a guiding image.
- Guiding Image: _____

If no specific image comes to mind use a cascading fountain.

Skills Enhanced/Developed: Crossing mid-line, fluid movement, greater coordination between left and right sides of body, mental discipline.

Journal Response: Did the addition of a guiding image help the execution of the movement? Elaborate. What did you notice about your breathing? Your structural integrity? Unnecessary muscle tension? If the chosen image does not help, continue to develop one that does. Suggestions are: a fountain, pulling taffy, a rubber band, etc. Notes:

9.9 Moving Through The Space
* As space permits

**CAUTION If you are dizzy or feel unstable with your eyes closed, place yourself where you can either feel a chair against the backs of your legs, or where you can place your hands on the back of a chair, table, desk, etc.

The goal is to recognize kinesthetic awareness and maintain structural integrity. Facilitator instructs participants to:

1. "Begin to walk freely within the parameters." Approximately 20 seconds.
2. "Stop (standing or sitting) in a neutral position. Close your eyes." **
3. "Intentionally focus on your internal awareness and make any slight adjustments necessary.
4. "Open your eyes and begin to walk through the space again, maintaining any adjustments made." 20 seconds.
5. "Turn 90* and continue walking. Stop. turn 45* and continue walking."
6. "Repeat steps 2 and 3."
7. "Open your eyes and begin to walk through the space with a comfortable stride."

8. "Slow your pace and lengthen your stride."
9. "Repeat steps 2 and 3. Were you able to maintain structural integrity? If so, open your eyes and maintain either the pace or length of stride or both. If not, resume your habitual gate."
10. Allow the participants to continue 10 or 20 seconds

Skills Developed/Enhanced: physical perception, kinesthetic awareness, spatial awareness

Journal Response: Was it easy or difficult to incorporate the slight adjustments? What superfluous movements were you able to correct? How did the addition of specific turns effect you? Where did your gaze rest? Did your gaze change when you altered your stride? How? Notes:"

Ten

10. Re-Assessment

To be facilitated as the initial assessment, noting any additional challenges.

Mental Flexibility

- Participants stand or sit in a circle in a neutral position.
- Exercise is silent.
- Participants toss and catch a 12 to 14inch ball without a break in rhythm.
- If no facilitator, the group designates a participant to begin and end the exercise.
- If additional challenge added, specify here

_____

Skills Assessed
- mental flexibility
- interdependence"

Skill Level	Specification	Point Value
Essential	Continually toss and catch the ball	1 point
Adequate	Continually toss and catch while maintaining silence	2 points
Proficient	Continually toss and catch, maintain silence, hold neutral position	3 points
Superior	Continually toss and catch, maintain silence, hold neutral position, concentrate on activity while increasing tempo	4 points
Excellent	Continually toss and catch, maintain silence, hold neutral position, concentrate on activity while increasing tempo until a predetermined alert signifies completion of exercise	5 points

A predetermined alert may be as simple as the facilitator's calling "stop" after an agreed time."

Participant Log

Participants Name	Date	Point value 1st Assessment	Point value 2nd Assessment	% Diff.

Physical Perception

- Measure 15 feet or more.
- Mark beginning point A and ending point B.
- Participant estimates the number of steps from point A to point B.
- Facilitator counts the number of steps actually taken as participant increases cognitive load (CL) by repeating aloud a known passage or performing mental math calculations while walking.
- Compare participant's estimated number of steps to facilitator's count of actual steps. Difference between estimate and actual determines skill level.

- If additional challenge added, specify here

  _____

Skills Assessed

- Awareness of external environment
- Structural integrity

Skill Level	Specifications	Point Value	
Essential	Estimated number of steps from point A to point B is 20% of actual number of steps	1 point	
Adequate	Estimated number of steps from point A to point B is between 20% and 40% of actual number of steps and gaze remains on point B	2 points	
Proficient	Estimated number of steps from point A to point B is between 40% and 60% of actual number of steps, gaze remains on point B, and gait is steady	3 points	

Skill Level	Specifications	Point Value
Superior	Estimated number of steps from point A to point B is between 60% and 80% of actual number of steps, gaze remains on point B, and gait is steady	4 points
Excellent	Estimated number of steps from point A to point B is between 80% and 100% of actual number of steps, gaze remains on point B, and gait is steady	5 points

Participant Log

Participants Name	DATE	DISTANCE	Est.	Actual	% Diff.

Kinesthetic Awareness

-

- Participants stand or sit in a neutral position.
- Each raises both arms above head, palms facing in.

- Count 1: participant's right shoulder rotates forward, lowering extended arm to the side, palm facing down.
- Count 2: participant's arm movement continues counterclockwise as right arm bends at elbow and palm passes chin, hand rotates turning palm to right ear.
- Count 3: participant's right arm extends straight up lengthening, return to starting position.
- Left arm mirrors movement, but begins after right arm reaches count 1.
- If additional challenge added, specify here
  _____

Skills Assessed
- Coordination
- Flow

- Crossing midline

Skill Level	Specifications	Point Value
Essential	Arms move in unison	1 point
Adequate	Arms move in unison for 3 distinct moves	2 points
Proficient	Arms alternate movement for 3 distinct moves	3 points
Superior	Arms alternate movement for 3 distinct moves, and *flow* is continuous	4 points
Excellent	Arms alternate movement for 3 distinct moves, flow is continuous, and specific direction of the palm is correct	5 points

Participant Log

Participant Name	Date	Point value 1st Assessment	Point value 2nd Assessment	% Diff.

If **all** participants achieve excellent in mental flexibility or **individually** for physical perception and/or kinesthetic awareness, the facilitator should increase the cognitive load by adding additional challenges.

Glossary

Blocking-The term used to describe movements on a stage.

Cognitive load-The amount of mental energy being used to complete a task.

Contracting awareness-Awareness which decreases.

Coordination-Synchronizing of opposing body parts.

Core strength-Intercostal muscles which aid breathing and support the skeleton.

Crossing the mid-line-Any physical activity which moves across the midline of the body.

Diaphragm-Muscle used for natural breathing.

Diaphragmatic breathing-Breathing that intentionally engages the diaphragm.

Dynamic-Progressive change.

Expanding awareness-Awareness which increases.

Facilitator-One who guides and observes others.

Feldenkrais method-applied method of movement therapy. See Moshe Feldenkrais.

Flow-energy unimpeded by tension.

Focus-Mental energy directed to a task.

Gate-Term used to describe a way of habitual walking, and may be intentionally altered.

Gaze-Term used to describe habitual line of sight, and may be intentionally altered.

General memory-information or activity relegated to an instinctive response.

Goal-The desired outcome

Grounded-The feeling of being rooted.

Guiding image-A detailed mental image which informs physical movement.

Improvisation-Training method for actors which requires mental flexibility.

Interdependence-Mutual reliance

Intonation-The natural rise and fall of the pitch of the voice when properly supported with the breath.

Isolate-Mentally focusing on a specific movement while physically performing that movement.

Kinesthetic awareness-Term describing the internal awareness of physical movements.

Mental flexibility-The ability to move the thought process from the right to the left hemisphere of the brain.

Midline-Movement that moves from one side of the body to the other side.

Mind/body connection-The theory that cognitive thought about a physical movement has an effect on the physical manifestation of that movement.

Moshe Feldenkrais-Israeli physicist who died in 1984 and developed the self-titled method of movement. See Feldenkrais method.

Neutral position-Standing or sitting position with legs and arms uncrossed and weight equal on right and left.

Participant-One who is active.

Physical perception-improved dynamic relationship between the participant, gravity, and society.

Structural integrity-Maintaining optimum posture.

Working memory-Manipulation of newly acquired information.

Appendix A : Numerical Exercise List

1. Warm up: Any exercise beginning the lesson.

2. Gaze: Connecting your habitual gaze to its effect on physical perception.

3. Ball Toss: Mental flexibility exercise.

4. Coordination/Flow: Kinesthetic awareness development.

5. Moving Meditation: Mental and physical exercise.

6. Moving Meditation: Detail: Specific alignment and sequencing of the moving meditation exercise.

7. Breathing Basics: Strengthening kinesthetic awareness

8. Blocking; Developing the ability to view personal environment from a first-person perspective.

9. Moving Through The Space: Physical perception exercise.

10. Sensory Recall: Memory recall focused on sensory input.

11. Add on group improvisation: Mental flexibility exercise.

12. Imagination Development: Engaging mental energy to recall details.

Appendix B: Additional Challenges

<u>Lesson One</u>

1.1 Warm Up

- Increase number of items to recall, i.e. name, occupation, marital status. All three items relate to the person.
- Once a connection is made between names, add an unrelated item, i.e., color or number. How can you relate seemingly un-relatable objects to aid in memory?
- Use words that begin with a common letter, numbers, number sequences, topics of particular interest or news items, whatever the group finds mentally stimulating.

1.2 Gaze

- Vary distance
- Vary the path.

1.3 Ball Toss
- Add a second or third ball.
- Begin to make up a story, one sentence or phrase at a time, to test ability to logically follow the thread of a story. The more active and descriptive the story, the easier to conjure images in your imagination, making the story easier to recall.
- Add a physical movement after you toss the ball.
- Linguistic challenges such as: animals, vegetables, or foods beginning with a specific letter of the alphabet, types of weather, etc.

<u>Lesson Two</u>

2.4 Coordination/Flow
- Facing another participant, mirror movement
- Facing another participant, stagger the start.

Coordination/Flow plus guiding image

Suggestions for guiding image when working in pairs: paddle wheel, one participant imagines the wheel, the other participant imagines the water as it moves through the wheel.

Lesson Five

5.10 Sense Recall

- Recall a daily activity
- Recall a stressful activity
- Re-enact a daily activity for the group. Is the group able to identify what the activity is? How much detail did you recall for yourself?

5.11 Add on Group Improvisation

A bank

A park

A beach

A busstop

Lesson Six

6.13 Mirror

- Without discussion, change lead each time the facilitator claps.
- Without discussion, begin the exercise.

Resources

Learning H.O.W. to Age™

www.quickmedical.com

De Bono, Edward. Lateral Thinking. Harper Collins ebook ed. December 2011. ISBN: 978-0-062-04327-6

Feldenkrais, Moshe. Awareness Through Movement. Harper Collins paperback edition, 1990.

Carter, Rita. Mapping the Mind. University of California Press, 1999.

Restak, Richard M.D. Otimizing Brain Fitness. The Great Courses, The Teaching Company, 2011.

Spolin, Viola. Improvisations for Theatre. Northwestern University Press, 1963

Early, Mary Beth Early, Lorraine Williams Pedretti Editors. Occupational Therapy, 5th ed. Mosby, Inc., 1981

Works Cited
Emerging: From Coma to Presence

Campbell, Joseph, and Bill D. Moyers. *The Power of Myth.*

New York: Doubleday, 1988. Print.

Companions in Christ: a small-group experience in spiritual formation; Gerrit Scott Dawson ...[et al.]. Nashville, Tennessee; Upper Room Books; 2001.

Feldenkrais, Moshe. *Awareness Through Movement.* United States of .America: HarperCollins Publisher, 1990 (softcover edition).

Estefan, Gloria. *Into the Light.* Sony, 1991.

Hatch, Edwin, 1835-1889. Hymn #420. The United Methodist Hymnal: Book of United Methodist Worship. Nashville, TN: United Methodist House, 1989. Print.

Hill, Gerald N., and Kathleen Hill. Nolos plain-English law dictionary. Berkeley, CA, Nolo, 2009.

Lewis, C.S. *Of Other worlds: essays and stories* San Diego: Harvest Books, 2000.

Lewis, C. S. *Surprised by Joy*. United Kingdom: Geoffrey Bles (UK) and Harcourt Brace (US), 1955. Paperback.

"Rudolf Otto's The Idea of the Holy 1: Summary." Bytrentsacred.co.uk. Web. 29 Feb. 2016.

The Holy Bible: Containing the Old and New Testaments with the Apocryphal/Deuterocanonical Books: New Revised Standard Version. KJV ed. New York: Oxford UP, 1989. Print. 1 Corinthians 13:12, John 10:10 and 15:5, Philippians 2:6-7.

The Holy Bible, Containing the Old and New Testaments. New York: T. Nelson & Sons, 1901. KJV. Print. Corinthians 13:12, John 14:18-19, 15:4, 1 Kings 19:12, Romans 8:38-39, 1Thessalonians 5:17.

The Holy Bible, New International Version: Containing the Old Testament and the New Testament. East Brunswick, NJ: International Bible Society, 1997. Print. 1 Corinthians 12:27. Galatians. 6:2.

Merton, Thomas. *Thoughts in solitude*. Farrar, Straus, and Giroux, 2000.

Voices from the past: Puritan devotional readings. Edinburgh: Banner of Truth Trust, 2009. Print.

"What is the Glasgow Coma Sale." Traumatic Brain Injury - TBI & Head Injury Resource BrainLine.org. N.p., n.d. Web. 28 Feb. 2017. <http://www.brainline.org/>.

courses.washington.edu/.../descendingpathway

gravitycenter.com/practice/breath-prayer/

http://www.beliefnet.com/Prayers/Protestant/Morning/ Morning Prayer.aspx#R8VrHXV3oAeA2JZq.99

http://www.brainyquote.com/quotes/quotes/r/raybradbur140827.html

http://genius.com/The-beatles-lucy-in-the-sky-with-diamonds-lyrics.

http://psychology.about.com/od/psychosocialtheories

nind.nih.org

About the Author

Angela Deaton Dortch earned an M.F.A. from University of Louisville in 1992. She was a contributor to The New Psalms Project at St. Paul United Methodist Church and wrote and produced plays for children and young adults. As a result of her successful rehabilitation, she developed a participatory wellness program--Learning H.O.W. to Age--that includes exercises involving many of the creative skills she learned from movement, dance, and acting. She lives in Louisville Kentucky with her husband of 35 years. To discover more about the wellness program or to reach the author email: Dortch5209@gmail.com.